Finding Wholeness Through the Science of Connecting

Drawing on the author's decades of experience in social work, this book introduces readers to a systems approach to reconnecting in a complex, disconnected world applying the *Dynamics of Life* model.

The systems sciences allow us to explore how we connect and disconnect, which can help us find ourselves again. Through his *Dynamics of Life* model, Victor MacGill presents this science in a simple, understandable way so that practitioners can build their skills and learn methods to apply with clients. The beginning of the book introduces theoretical concepts, such as complex adaptive systems, living systems and 4e cognition. The second half introduces tools for how to manage conflict and to reconnect and rebuild relationships with ourselves, individuals, family and community. The book is a manual for reconnecting ourselves to ourselves, others and the world to realise our greater potential.

An essential resource in a disconnected and fragmented world, this book is for anyone in the helping professions, including counsellors, psychologists, social workers and coaches and so forth.

Victor MacGill has over forty years' experience as a social worker in the field of criminal justice, specialising in family violence and has been studying the systems sciences for thirty years. Victor is the New Zealand contact for ANZSYS, the Australia New Zealand regional branch of the International Society for the Systems Sciences (ISSS), as well as Co-chair of Critical Systems Special Integration Group of ISSS. He has developed a model called the *Dynamics of Life*™ that describes the processes of life and many varied levels of functioning that has many practical applications in a wide range of situations.

Finding Wholeness Through the Science of Connecting

An Introduction to the *Dynamics of Life* Model

Victor MacGill

Routledge
Taylor & Francis Group

LONDON AND NEW YORK

Designed cover image: Victor MacGill

First published 2025
by Routledge
4 Park Square, Milton Park, Abingdon, Oxon OX14 4RN

and by Routledge
605 Third Avenue, New York, NY 10158

Routledge is an imprint of the Taylor & Francis Group, an informa business

© 2025 Victor MacGill

British Library Cataloguing-in-Publication Data
A catalogue record for this book is available from the British Library

Library of Congress Cataloging-in-Publication Data
Names: MacGill, Victor, author.
Title: Finding wholeness through the science of connecting : an introduction to the dynamics of life model / Victor MacGill.
Description: Abingdon, Oxon ; New York, NY : Routledge, 2025. | Includes bibliographical references and index. | Contents: Connecting and disconnecting -- Living systems -- Further concepts -- Human systems -- Changing behaviour -- Extended cognitive behaviour theory -- Human relationships -- Further concepts and strategies -- Culture and community -- Reconnecting. |
Identifiers: LCCN 2024040600 (print) | LCCN 2024040601 (ebook) | ISBN 9781032876344 (hbk) | ISBN 9781032876337 (pbk) | ISBN 9781003533641 (ebk)
Subjects: LCSH: Social interaction. | Social systems. | System theory | Cognitive science. | Mind and body.
Classification: LCC HM1111 .M33 2025 (print) | LCC HM1111 (ebook) | DDC 302--dc23/eng/20241028
LC record available at https://lccn.loc.gov/2024040600
LC ebook record available at https://lccn.loc.gov/2024040601

ISBN: 978-1-032-87634-4 (hbk)
ISBN: 978-1-032-87633-7 (pbk)
ISBN: 978-1-003-53364-1 (ebk)

DOI: 10.4324/9781003533641

Typeset in Sabon
by SPi Technologies India Pvt Ltd (Straive)

Contents

Preface

Many years ago, I decided that our continued willingness to use violence to resolve difference was the biggest impediment to human evolution. That began a journey with two threads. My working life led me to twenty years in the criminal justice area, working as a probation officer, a non-violence programme facilitator, and, more recently, a family violence facilitator. The second thread was discovering Systems Theory, the science of connecting and disconnecting, which provided me with a framework to understand the underlying dynamics of human behaviour.

Since we are all different, conflict is inherent in human interactions. We can, however, learn to work with difference in ways that minimise harm and generate positive outcomes. Becoming more aware of our darker side and our capacity for violence allows us to make better decisions so we become more effective beings. Peace is not an endpoint to be reached; it is a process of healing and becoming.

I was raised by foster parents in the Anglican Church in Nelson, New Zealand. I remember picking up something from the minister's house when I was about nine years old. I was met by his wife, who asked me if I believed in God. I knew the right answer was "Yes, of course". I walked away wondering if I really did.

I went to university to learn science. I also encountered Māori culture, which revealed a fully valid alternative way of seeing the world. It was full of gods, ancestors, and a deep connectedness to each other and the natural world. A different mythology revealed an open window to other ways of knowing. My birth mother was a Theosophist, and my birth father a Buddhist. My mother died when I was six. My birth father retired and went to live in a Buddhist monastery in Japan, but he later returned to New Zealand, where I looked after him for about two years until his death. We talked about Buddhism. His style is Theravada, an earlier form, whereas my contact with Buddhism has mainly been with Tibetan Buddhism.

I see the world through many lenses, each giving me a different perspective. I have been influenced by New Age beliefs and active in Men's work.

My spirituality has become far more practical as I grow older; it has become more about being a good person and living a good life.

Systems Theory was the connector that brought all the threads together, opening a pathway to reconnect back to myself and my world. What I found to be *God*, if I needed a word, was the underlying patterns of cohesion that hold life together. Good and evil, order and chaos, moved from being opposites, where one should be eliminated, to two ends of a tension arising from one reality to be experienced. Difference and error are always present. When the tensions fall out of balance, abuse and violence often arise.

I am extremely fortunate in that I have met and known most of the present-day systems scientists mentioned in this book at various conferences around the world before and after completing my PhD. I also met family members or past students of many of the pioneers who have since died. It helps keep me up with the cutting-edge of systems research.

The Māori culture of New Zealand has systems wisdom woven all through it. Māori people retain the connection to their family (whānau) and tribe (iwi), their ancestors (tūpuna), and the natural world in which they live. Since this is the indigenous culture I am most familiar with, the majority of the examples of indigenous ways of being used in this book come from the New Zealand Māori.

I owe a deep debt of gratitude to all the clients I have worked with over many years. It has been very much a two-way process, where I learn at least as much as they do. It has provided me with countless opportunities to develop the ideas and techniques that have had a significant positive impact on many people's lives. Often it is the simplest techniques that bring about the greatest change. The simplicity of the 1-10 Anger Scale hides the power it gives people to monitor their behaviour and realise they can have control over themselves and their decisions. This book is intended as a guidebook to share the wisdom I have gained with a wider audience. I welcome you to a journey of learning and discovery. Travel well!

Introduction

As Odysseus returned to his homeland, he had to sail his ship between Scylla, a six-headed monster, and Charybdis, a whirlpool. Sailing too close to either spelt destruction. We similarly navigate our lifepath through order and chaos, autonomy and connectedness, unity and diversity, and more. When we drift too far either way or see them as opposites and choose one over the other, we lose balance and pay the price. Indeed, passing between Scylla and Charybdis cost Odysseus six men.

Whenever we fall out of balance and become disconnected, we create suffering and violence. It may be physical, emotional, mental, or even cultural. While science has brought us so many of the wonders of our age, its focus on breaking things down into smaller and smaller categories to understand the world has meant it misses how everything connects. We all suffer from being disconnected from ourselves, other people, and our environment. The world has become seen as disconnected parts to be used for profit irrespective of the harm caused.

This book describes the journey out of disconnection back to wholeness guided by systems wisdom. Systems Theory is the science of how things connect and disconnect. Rather than replacing reductionist science, it expands what science can offer. I use the term systems wisdom because we must go beyond intellectual knowledge to a way of life we feel in our bones and in our hearts that brings us home to ourselves. Many indigenous peoples retain a sense of connection the rest of the world has lost. As an example, the Māori people of New Zealand say, "'Ko au te whenua, ko te whenua, ko au", which means "I am the land, and the land is me".

To harm the other is to harm ourselves. To heal ourselves is to heal others. This book explores how life could be if we choose to reconnect our wounded parts, taking back our role as stewards of our environment, and caring for ourselves and others. The concepts, tools, and techniques presented in this book are easily useable by people like you and the many hundreds of clients I have worked with to gain greater control of their lives.

Although there have been systems thinkers all through history, systems became formalised in the twentieth century. Ludwig von Bertalanffy, Norbert Wiener, Alexander Bogdanov, Henri Poincaré and others worked in the first half of the twentieth century, but Systems and Cybernetics really took off after World War II, laying the foundation for understanding general systems concepts like feedback loops, isomorphy (that differing complex systems have similar underlying characteristics), and nested systems that hold true for all complex systems. Complexity Theory arose as a science when computers became powerful enough to do the necessary computations, so there is no single systems science. Ironically, it is a system of concepts, models, and theories that connect together. Systems Theory has made real advances, but it has not had the level of recognition by mainstream science to put those ideas into practice in a world that sorely needs them.

I found systems in the mid-1990s, and it changed my life. It linked my spiritual longing to feel a wholeness with a science that made sense and provided a pathway that I now offer you as both a map to navigate the future and also specific tools to help on the journey.

I developed a conceptual framework to describe the functioning of living systems called the *Dynamics of Life* model, which is the central concept repeated throughout the book. The core of the model is a diagram that describes the processes that give rise to life from a single-celled creature, to an animal, to a human. From there, it describes social processes from two people in a partnership through to nations vying for power and influence at a global level. It even describes ecological, economic, and political systems. It covers the biological, and the psychological, which includes emotion and thinking, the social realm of interacting humans, and points to a spiritual realm in the future.

The layers of biological, psychological, and social are not separate but intensely interconnected and influence each other. Each new level arises out of the previous level, relying on it as a foundation that adds capacity and complexity to living systems. Each new level also brings its challenges and pitfalls. Cognitive mapping allows us to understand and manage our life; however, because error is inherent, our maps will be incomplete. You will learn to read patterns in your actions and others that enable wiser responses. To read this book just as a collection of tools and techniques would be to miss the real magic. I hope that as you read the various models and tools, you are drawn beyond the lines of text to a new, more connected way of feeling and making sense of the world about you. It is a way of being.

The writing of this book has been driven by the desire to make the understandings and techniques that have enriched my life and many others available to a wider audience than those I have worked with personally. I have borrowed heavily from the ideas of others. My contribution is distilling and condensing their ideas in ways that I hope make them more easily understood and usable.

Chapter 1

Connecting and Disconnecting

Victor MacGill

Introduction

We live in an age of enormous conflict. We are taught to see ourselves and the world as full of separate, disconnected elements. Inequality and greed have risen to extreme levels, politics is more polarised, the threat of nuclear war is as close as ever, and we have plundered our planet to the point that catastrophic climate change could make the Earth unhabitable.

We are disconnected at the very core of our being, and also at every level of our being. Despite our best intentions, that disconnection has led to inconceivable ongoing acts of violence and abuse. There is a pathway we can each choose that reconnects these disconnected parts. We can embark on a journey to heal the wounds of the past and create better futures. It is not an easy path to pursue because the old path is so familiar. We will enlist the help of systems wisdom to provide a framework to come to know ourselves, others, and the world, that can help us navigate the perilous territory before us.

Mainstream science uses reductionist techniques to divide the world into categories and separate parts. Reductionism has brought so many wonderful technological innovations and systems science does not say reductionism is wrong, but if it is regarded as the only way to look at the world, it is incomplete. Systems has all the rigour and precision of mainstream science, but looks at the wider picture of the parts and their relationship to each other. You may find Systems Theory given different labels. There is, for example, a significant overlap between Systems Theory, Cybernetics, and Complexity Theory.

In this work I use the term systems wisdom because we need more than an intellectual framework to reconnect our lives. Systems wisdom becomes a way of being in the world. It is not systems wisdom until you feel it in your bones and heart. Many indigenous traditions retain their connectedness and have much to teach us.

Life has arisen out of the tensions between order and chaos. While we maintain that balance, we are productive and flourish. If we tip too far into

DOI: 10.4324/9781003533641-1

chaos, however, we slip into anarchy and unpredictability; similarly, if we tip too far towards order, we become rigid and inflexible. Either way, we create suffering. We also need to balance autonomy and connectivity. In the same way, we can be too focused on ourselves and our individual needs and desires, or too focused on fitting in with others and their desires. The balance is always like that of a tightrope walker[1] continuously readjusting the balance to enable walking forward on the rope. When we cannot handle the disorder, we try and pass it on to others. We might dump our anger on somebody else, who must then handle it. In this manner disorder moves around like a hot potato.

Central to the journey of healing is a willingness to look at our darker sides and acknowledge that despite our best intentions, you and I, either knowingly or otherwise, are capable of much greater abuse and violence than we would like to admit. We do it in obvious ways that hurt the people around us and in not-so-obvious ways, such as the violence and suffering hidden in the production of the consumer goods we buy and take for granted.

There is a saying that goes:

When we can't find love, we make do with power.

We seek to meet our needs by connecting with others through supporting, caring, and cooperating. Sometimes we find that, even with our best efforts, we consciously or unconsciously feel our needs have not been met by sharing power with others and shift to meet our needs by using power over them. It is surprisingly easy to fall into abuse or violence, often inflicting our greatest injury on those closest to us.

There is a well-known Pogo cartoon that simply says, "I have seen the enemy, and he is us". So often we reject the things in ourselves we would rather avoid and project them onto others. Until we have the insight and the courage to honestly look at ourselves and accept our human nature, we will perpetuate the very violence we claim to despise. The challenge is to undertake the perilous journey to explore our inner nature. You will not eliminate conflict or even violence from your life, but this book will help you find better ways to live with the darker side of your nature.

As much as the foundation of civilisation is based on people collaborating and trusting that others will act fairly, violence (or the threat of it) has often been the source of social compliance. In many animal and human societies, "Do as I say or else" has often led to compliance through the threat of fear. Paradoxically, such a group often gains a fitness advantage over other more peaceful groups. It could be argued, in fact, that the fear of violence lies at the root of human civilisation. Indeed, Max Weber[2] defined the sovereign of a state as being the institution that claims the legitimate use of violence over its citizens. The sovereign asserts the power to use the final means of maintaining control.

Today, we tend to see the world as being filled with separate, unconnected parts that do not impact upon one another. Each part is given a monetary value and then traded for profit, seemingly irrespective of the impact on people and the environment. All the many crises we see in this troubled world, whether they are ecological or economic, related to political instability, or the threat of nuclear war, arise from seeing the world as full of separate parts made into commodities.

We humans have a strange relationship with violence. While we abhor it and are horrified when it arises in our lives, many of us pay actually money to witness violence in a boxing ring or on a sports field. When the goody shoots and kills the baddy in a movie, the feeling is not one of repulsion and disgust at the death of a human being, but rather the notion of completion and of justice having been served. Similarly, soldiers in war, who perpetrated extreme acts of violence on other individuals, are hailed as heroes, with statues erected to commemorate their deeds.

Conflict cannot be eradicated from our lives and our continued existence on this planet is under threat but that does not mean our prospects of living good, true lives are in vain. Indeed, the challenge is living with a capacity for violence and harm and choosing not to use it. There are definite skills and abilities you can develop to resolve difference and conflict in more harmonious ways.

Systems is interested in the relationships between the parts, and how they balance their interactions. A forest has many competing life forms which live off one another, yet forests can remain in balance for thousands of years. We have much to learn from the underlying patterns, trade-offs, and tensions in a forest.

What I have written so far might seem to give the impression that connecting is good and disconnecting is bad, but the reality is much more subtle than that. There are times to disconnect. For example, a child must eventually leave home, leaves fall in autumn, and people die or move away. Sometimes it is just too toxic to stay connected. Disconnecting becomes the right thing to do. In the words of the Māori people of New Zealand:

Mate atu he tētēkura, ara mai he tētēkura.

As one fern frond dies, another rises to take its place. Disconnecting outside these times is usually harmful to a living system.

This book sets out to provide a practical manual, with two particular goals. The first is to use systems wisdom to understand life so you can make better sense of your experience and thus know how to act more effectively. The second is to provide specific tools and strategies for you to put in place to help on the healing journey of reconnecting.

This chapter follows a pattern repeated throughout the book. It starts with a general introduction to the theme to be discussed. A series of concepts and ideas follows that lays the foundation for the main idea of the chapter. Exercises and tools are included that can be used to develop skills and understanding arising out of the theme of the chapter.

The *Dynamics of Life* model is used as a framework through this book to understand the process of life and how it is manifested at each level. Once this is in place, we will see how living systems can go wrong and how to build effective, wholesome ways of behaving.

Our starting point is to learn some key ideas and concepts of systems wisdom which can be applied to all complex systems. Later chapters will focus on living, human, and then social systems, building towards a presentation of the *Dynamics of Life* model that shows how they all fit together. These basic concepts will allow us to build a picture of a healthy system, and then an unhealthy system, demonstrating how we have become so disconnected. Our starting point is to ask a seemingly simple question: "What is a system?"

What is a System?

Our world is full of systems. These include, among many others, postal systems, educational systems, body systems, planetary systems, computer systems, government systems, and more. A person is a complete system made up of all the body organs and parts, which are complete systems in themselves, connecting and coordinating into one being. A family is a system. Each member has their own identity, but they come together to form a unity that supports and cares for each other. Their bonds hold them together as they live out their individual roles. A football team is a system in which the players interact and communicate with each other for a common purpose. By contrast, a pile of rocks is not a system. Individual rocks do not interact in a meaningful way.[3] We can say:

> *A system is a collection of parts that connect together to create a new whole that can do things that the individual parts could not do alone.*[4]

Some systems are simple, such as a water pump. You can easily tell how it works and predict what will happen when you use it. Other things, like a jet airliner, are more complicated. Thousands of parts all fit together, but they are still highly predictable. Yet other systems, like a fire or the weather, are largely chaotic in nature; they have some predictability, but relatively little. Finally, there are complex systems, where the balance of order and chaos opens new possibilities. Anything alive is complex. Since our topic is human violence, we are more interested in complex systems that are reasonably predictable in some ways but which can respond in ways we do not expect. Any of the system types above can devolve into deep chaos and disorder.[5]

Systems connect and disconnect, creating patterns that enable them to maintain their existence. The parts have boundaries that separate them from each other. As soon as they set up a boundary to make them distinct, they have an individual perspective through which they see the world and form relationships connecting the other parts.

There is a tension in every system between the desire to be an individual and different (autonomy), and the desire to belong and connect with others (connectivity). I must constrain what I want to do in order to fit the rules of the group. If I focus more on my own needs and desires, I tend to defocus from those of my group. Life is a dynamic ongoing rebalancing of being separate and being connected. If there is too much autonomy, the whole system loses cohesion as each part just does its own thing. By contrast, if there is too much connectivity, the parts become rigid and controlled. A good balance ensures cohesion and flexibility.

The parts of a system must have a reason to come together. They cooperate because they can achieve more by cooperating than by remaining alone. Two people can carry a heavy load more easily together than they can separately, but cooperating means forgoing some personal desires. While I gain by cooperating in shifting firewood with my neighbour that we will share, I have less time to fix my car. The gains of having a pile of firewood must be greater than the gains of fixing my car sooner.

Complex systems have fundamental characteristics that help us understand what happens as the parts of a system interact together. You will become aware of underlying tensions inherent in all complex systems that enable them to exist.[6]

Boundaries

When we make a distinction, we create a boundary. In the world, some of these are obvious. For example, if I am in a deep hole, the boundary is clear because what I can do in the hole is very different from what I can do outside the hole. However, most of the boundaries in the world are created in our minds. We create categories that include similar things, but there are different ways of dividing things up. A pack of cards can be divided by number, suit, colour, picture cards, and numbered cards. The way I choose to divide my world determines how I make-sense of my world and also how I act in it.

As soon as a part of a system is defined, what is inside the boundary takes on an individual identity. It has its own perspective on its situation and its own purpose. That identity will shape the way the part or system interacts with others. We build our sense of identity by comparing ourselves to others. I look at myself and see who I am like and who I am different from. I find myself to be tall, male, balding, outgoing, and less organised than I might like to think I am.

As soon as two parts interact, a relationship is formed. I constantly respond to your responses to me, and in the same way you respond to my responses to you. It is like partners dancing, constantly adjusting themselves, while remaining aware of the other and adjusting to their adjustment as well. Neither is in charge, but both can influence the interaction. If they both follow the rules of how to interact, we witness a beautiful dance. Such chain reactions are called *recursive* interactions.

Boundaries both reveal and conceal. When I choose to see the world from a particular point of view, I can make sense of what I experience and bring it to light, but the cost is that other potential and equally valid ways of seeing the world recede into the background. Where I lay my boundary establishes who or what I include within my circle and who or what remains outside. Having wide boundaries risks allowing toxic elements to get close, while keeping boundaries too close excludes those who could be helpful and supportive.

Difference is especially noticeable at boundaries, meaning conflict and violence can tend to arise at boundary points. The more aware we are of our boundaries, the more likely we can find ways to reduce boundary conflict from escalating to unnecessary conflict and violence.

Al Gore spoke of an *Inconvenient Truth* about climate change, but living systems exist by *Convenient Untruths*. A boundary is usually only something created in our mind; without that boundary, however, nothing can be perceived as separate. There is no me and no you. Because of the boundaries, we can have a useful dialogue that connects us and allows us to act effectively in the world. Money is only bits of paper or numbers on a computer screen, but because everyone acts as if it is real, it becomes useful. The more you are aware of the untruths behind the appearance of our world and how they work, the better you will be able to make effective choices.

As we experience life, reaching conclusions about ourselves and the world, we create a mental map of ourselves and the world in which we live. A paper map represents things in the world and their relationships which enable us to navigate the terrain to reach our destinations. We similarly have cognitive maps that map who I am, who other people are, my relationship with them, and how I perceive life. By checking my cognitive map and comparing it to my world, just as we do with a paper map or a map on our phone, we work out how to navigate our world and achieve the goals we set. The map shows my boundaries and categories and what I think is safe and unsafe.

The cognitive map is never perfect, but the more accurately it maps the world as it is, the more useful it will become. Religions and philosophies are a form of cultural mapping that present a meaningful coherent way of seeing the world, but each one is still only one way of viewing the world.

As we interact, we create culture as shared ways of seeing the world. We place shared boundaries around how we agree to act together for mutual benefit. Each generation passes on the shared ways as a culture for the next generation. We share language, customs, and ways of knowing. We inherit most of our boundaries from the people and society around us. Just as we shaped our culture, we, in turn, are shaped by our culture. We also inherit the errors and the trauma of previous generations. For many, other tribes were the enemy to be killed, slaves were to be used, and women were considered as property. Where and how we place boundaries, and who we include and exclude, matters.

The mere act of noticing your world establishes distinctions and boundaries, patterns, and likely future outcomes. Noticing is the first step to making changes in our lives. It is valuable to examine the boundaries you use to make sense of your world and the impact of seeing the world as you do.

Feedback

When we hear feedback from a friend, they are usually commenting on how we have handled a situation. We might, for example, be practising a golf swing. They watched and commented, and we use that information to change how we act next time. They might say we did well, and we will keep doing what we did; or they may give some advice on how to improve our golf swing. A loop is formed where we can continually improve our golf swing with each new piece of advice. We feed the output (the advice) back to become the input to know what to do next time, as shown in Figure 1.1. In the absence of feedback, there is no way to monitor and control our behaviour. Think about how feedback loops work in your life.

As a feedback loop starts circling around and around, there are two ways in which feedback can work. First, a positive feedback loop functions to make the output larger or smaller. If I put $1,000 in a bank account at 3% interest at the end of the year, I have $1,030, including the interest. In the second year, I earn interest on $1,030 instead of just $1,000. In the second year, I earn $30.90 interest, making a total of $1060.90. That 90 cents does not sound like much more, but If I continue over the years, my account grows exponentially. After 50 years, linear growth would add an extra $2,500, but compounded growth would give total earnings of $4,383.91. After 200 years, $1,000 becomes $369,355.82. This is depicted in Figure 1.2.

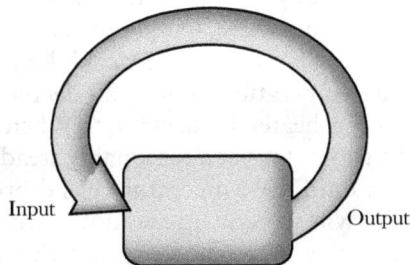

Input   Output

Figure 1.1 A basic feedback loop. The output coming out of the system is fed back as the input. If the output is the same as the input, the system will not change. If it differs, even a little, the system can change significantly after several cycles.

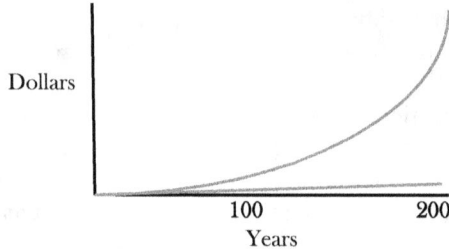

Figure 1.2 Exponential growth compared to linear growth.

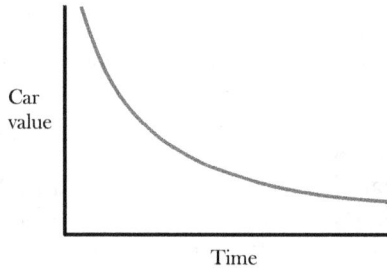

Figure 1.3 Decreasing exponential growth.

If I buy a car its value will decrease each year, as shown in Figure 1.3. If I bought it for $20,000 and it loses 5% per year, the next year it is worth $19,000. The next year it loses 5% of the $19,000, so the value decreases exponentially but this is still called a positive feedback loop.

An increasing bank account is good for the owner, but an exponential increase in cancer cells or pests is not. A loss of value for a car is not good for the owner, but a drop in the number of people with Covid is a good decreasing positive feedback loop.

Secondly, a negative feedback loop is one where the system works to keep itself in the same state. Our body uses many feedback loops to keep the heart, lungs, hormone levels, blood pressure, temperature, and more within survivable limits. A good example of a negative feedback loop is a thermostat. The goal is to keep the room temperature at, say, 20 degrees Celsius. If the temperature falls below 19.5 a heater is turned on. When it reaches 20.5, the heater is turned off. The room stays at a reasonably steady temperature. If the heater does not come on until the temperature has dropped to 15 and turns off at 25 the temperature will see-saw up and down within the range.

Often there is a time delay between the time a change happens, and the moments a response is put in place.[7] A car may approach a corner too fast because the driver delayed braking (Figure 1.4). Typically, they overreact, and the car heads for the other side of the road, so the driver recorrects again. The delay in braking caused the car to swing wildly over the road. At this

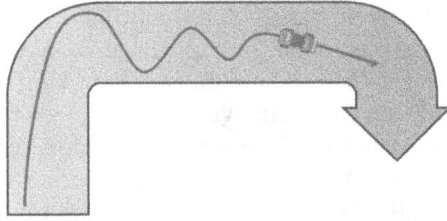

Figure 1.4 The delay between the driver noticing their position and reacting causes the car to sway back and forth across the road.

point the driver will either regain control of the car, or it will careen right off the road. A company may not notice that a product has stopped selling well, but developing a new product takes time. During that interval the market may have changed again, so time lags create instability. You will recognise events in your life when a time lag caused instability.

In real-life situations, feedback loops combine. Imagine pioneers settling on a newly discovered island. At first, everyone has plenty of land and resources. The population grows as an exponential positive feedback loop until they cover the whole island. At that point, people can no longer have all the land they want, and a negative feedback loop kicks in, slowing the rate of growth. There is a shift from exploring to exploiting.[8] People must make do with what they have available. That is not a problem for a while; as the population continues to increase, however, it becomes hard for people to meet their needs on smaller and smaller pieces of land. Eventually, it becomes unfeasible. Hopefully, the population will even off at the maximum sustainable level, but if it continues to increase, human life on the island will collapse.

System Archetypes

In 1972 Donella Meadows, Dennis Meadows, Jørgen Randers, and William Behrens published an important document called *The Limits to Growth*. In this publication they looked at global growth rates and saw our whole planet heading towards a fate similar to the island discussed above. Data collected since shows we are headed directly towards the more extreme negative scenarios they predicted fifty years ago.

The Limits to Growth is an example of a system archetype, describing common patterns of interacting feedback loops found in living systems or organisations.[9] Those most relevant to us are next described.

We sometimes have a problem with *shifting goals*. We have a target we would like to reach. Monitoring the feedback loops shows we have not met our target. Rather than finding ways to improve performance until the target is met, we lower our target. If this happens repeatedly, the target becomes so watered down as to be of no value. You might have an agreement to make 100 cakes a day for a company but only produce 90. Since they do not complain production slips to 70, and then 60, at which point the deal falls apart.

Escalation occurs when the recursive dance between two parties ratchets up in dangerous ways. The Cold War was a time of increased production of nuclear weapons in response to the fear that the other side would secretly build more weapons and leave this side vulnerable. Many arguments scale up from small disagreements that neither side is prepared to back down from.

Fixes not working is trying even harder when a strategy does not work. In the apt words of Russell Ackoff,

> The more efficient you are at doing the wrong thing, the wronger you become. It is much better to do the right thing wronger than the wrong thing righter. If you do the right thing wrong and correct it, you get better.

Complex adaptive systems exist in a complex environment, usually with other complex adaptive systems, so simple solutions are not possible. C. West Churchman writes of *wicked problems*.[10] In contrast to a tame problem like chess, where the rules are known and obeyed, the endpoint is known, and the possible moves are finite. Wicked problems have changing rules, no endpoint, and infinite possible outcomes. Most problems for living systems are wicked problems.

Everything in Life Winds Down

Everything in the universe tends to wind down over time.[11] A piece of fruit left out will rot, and mighty mountains will be worn flat. The measure of the disorder or chaos in a system is called *entropy*. The more wound down something is, the more entropy it possesses.

If I pour a coloured liquid into a container of water, the coloured liquid will slowly spread through the whole container until there is an even mix of one pale colour. Once the colour has spread there is no way to wind the clock backwards to how it was before. Time always moves forward, and disorder always increases over time.

A tornado or Jupiter's red spot are two examples of complex systems, but they only last as long as the conditions around them remain stable. They cannot keep themselves alive. Living systems are examples of complex adaptive systems because they can adapt their state to maintain their existence.

Complex Adaptive Systems

A complex adaptive system seems to break the rule that everything wears down. It does this by setting up flows of energy, matter, and information through its boundary, extracting what it needs from the flow to overcome the descent into disorder within the boundary. The extra energy allows it to maintain its internal functions and do work, such as seeking food or avoiding threats. It creates islands of order in a sea of chaos.

Matter brought into the system is metabolised in order to access its energy. Energy is extracted from food. The energy in plant foods is much more concentrated and useful than in sunlight and energy in an animal is even more condensed than in plants. Data is just measurements or a symbol or sign with no meaning, but it becomes information when there is an observable pattern. Information data is viewed in context. Information is further refined as knowledge, when we reveal meaning from the information to help us achieve a goal. Wisdom is the highest form, where knowledge is used to make effective decisions. My smart watch collects data such as how many steps I take and my heart rate. It becomes information when my watch displays average heart rates and compares the number of steps per day. I put the data in context by comparing the figures to target figures I have selected. I then find meaning in the figures as knowledge and I might deduce that I require more exercise. With wisdom, I develop a fitness plan.

If we receive a string of data that is always the same, there is no information in it. There is nothing new to learn. When we notice difference, we gain information from which we can extract meaning to create knowledge. Information tells us our heart rate has increased. This might give us knowledge, telling us, for example, we feel stressed. Wisdom tells us what to do to reduce the stress. Wisdom allows us to manage entropy much more effectively.

Not all the energy, matter, and information that flows into the system can be used, however. Some are expelled back into the environment and some stay trapped within the system to become toxic. Even though order was created inside the system, thereby lowering entropy, the overall level of disorder of the inside and outside combined still rises so the law of the universe winding down is still obeyed.

A refrigerator demonstrates how entropy works. It takes in electricity from the outside and uses it to reduce the heat inside and make it cold. It does that by moving heat outside; because some energy is lost, it creates more heat outside the fridge than cold inside, so overall entropy increases even if it decreases inside the refrigerator. If the refrigerator is turned off, it heats up inside to return to room temperature.

The one mathematical equation most people know is Einstein's $E = mc^2$, where E stands for energy, m stands for mass and c is the speed of light. This tells us that matter and energy are two forms of the same thing. One can be transformed into the other. Matter and energy also hold information. If an object is red, that redness is announced to the world merely by being. My body and everything I do with it generates information I project into the world just by being. Nothing can be other than it is even if it tries to hide it. Energy, matter, and information are highly interwoven.

Information degrades over time, just like energy and matter. It takes energy to maintain information, or it will eventually be lost. It might degrade in a number of different ways: through a mutation in DNA, a photograph fading over time, a hard drive deteriorating, or a gravestone becoming illegible. The loss of information has implications for the fitness of any complex system.

Complex adaptive systems must maintain the flow through their boundaries. Life stores energy, matter, and information to be used later when needed. Even that will end up being consumed or degraded. Living systems have repair mechanisms, to repair the damage; eventually, however, the repair mechanisms themselves will wear down. What remains will return to the earth just as the coloured liquid spreads through the container of water. Every living system has a limit to the amount of chaos it can contain and manage. When it reaches that limit, it must move the disorder elsewhere or it will start to destroy itself.

Complex adaptive systems take energy, matter, and information from the environment to create order within the boundary, thereby overcoming the disorder as seen in Figure 1.5. It's like we turn disorder into order at the front door while disorder creeps in the back door. The boundary and everything in it must be maintained and repaired. Skin cells change every two to three weeks and red blood cells every four months, but brain cells are not replaced when they no longer function. We retain the same organisation of the parts, so skin cells get replaced by skin cells, blood cells by blood cells, and so forth. This ongoing organisation enables us to maintain structural identity over time.[12] As long as there is space between the back door and the front door, life is sustained. As soon as the disorder cannot be overcome, the space for life collapses and the creature dies.

The parts in a living system need rules to guide how they act for the whole organism to remain coherent. In the simplest forms of life, the rules are "written" into the DNA structure. In a human being, there are belief systems that regulate and guide decision-making. Communities, companies, and nations have written laws and agreements that maintain order.

Figure 1.5 Complex adaptive systems create order to overcome the tendency to wind down, but more chaos enters from behind that also must be resolved.

Niklas Luhmann reminds us that a complex adaptive system is always less complex than the environment in which it lives since the environment is actually the rest of the universe. The system can never know everything about itself and its environment. This opens the space for error. We must, as Stuart Kauffman writes, "Act as if we know". We can only ever make our best guess, but we remain responsible for the consequences of our actions.

Complex adaptive systems come in several types. Some are living systems with a body. Some are social systems, which are made up of living systems but do not have a body, even if we might call them a corporate body. There are parts of a living system that are complex adaptive systems like our heart, lungs, and brain that have a defined physical form but do not have an autonomous existence in the same way as a person or animal has. You will also notice that a heart is made of cells, tissue, and glands, but a social system is not comprised of all the lower parts. One person is selected to be a colonel in the army, but the colonel is one person and does not have sergeants, corporals, and privates within his being in the way the heart is comprised of all the subsystems. They all share the attributes of complex adaptive systems, but each has unique manifestations. For the sake of brevity in this book, the term *living system* will often be used to include social systems to describe all these complex adaptive systems, but we need to keep these differences in mind. The *Dynamics of Life* model presented in Chapter 3 is designed to describe all these types of complex adaptive systems.

Healthy Systems

We can now identify the qualities of a healthy living system and, by contrast, the qualities of an unhealthy living system. This will shed light on how violence arises in living systems. We can now enumerate the qualities of a healthy system:

1 It can maintain its boundary
2 The parts are well-connected
3 It has balanced dynamic tensions
4 There is a steady flow of matter, energy, and information
5 It connects and disconnects appropriately
6 It maintains and repairs all its internal functions sufficiently
7 It can respond adequately to external influences
8 It balances autonomy and connectivity, cooperation, and competition
9 The parts that obey the rules adequately.

Unhealthy Systems

With a picture of a healthy system in mind, we can outline the qualities of an unhealthy system.

1 The boundaries cannot be maintained
2 The parts become disconnected
3 The dynamic tensions move out of balance
4 Flows of matter, energy, and information are disrupted
5 Inappropriate connecting and disconnecting
6 There is a lack of repair and maintenance
7 It fails to manage external influences
8 There is an imbalance of autonomy and connectivity, competition and cooperation
9 The parts significantly disobey the rule set.

From here, we can see action undertaken by a living system fits at some point on a continuum from health to unhealthy, or from love to violence. In general, the more we connect and come together, building and nourishing relationships, the more love arises. Humberto Maturana says that the natural state of a living organism is love.[13] The more we disconnect and break connections that should be maintained, the more violence arises. You now have a tool to look at the systems in your life and assess how healthy they are. We can now use our systems principles to gain an understanding of resolving difference.

Resolving Difference

A boundary arises where there is unresolved difference. Gregory Bateson writes of "difference that make a difference".[14] As I drive along the road, it does not make a difference whether a pedestrian I pass is wearing a green jacket or a red jacket, but it does matter whether the traffic light is green or red. W Ross Ashby[15] used the term *requisite variety*. If there is difference, there is variety. If the variety is requisite, it is necessary for what you wish to do. Thus, the traffic light colour makes a difference. If I fail to notice something critical or waste energy noticing irrelevant information, I will lose effectiveness and make errors that will increase conflict and the likelihood of violence.

A Systems Definition of Violence

Since a boundary marks a difference, conflict arises at boundaries. When that conflict is not well resolved, violence erupts at the boundary causing harm. Flows of energy, matter, and information cross boundaries to sustain the living system. Sometimes that flow is impeded or disrupted causing harm to the living system.

We can thus define violence as:

The invasion of a boundary or the disruption of a flow across a boundary.

Boundaries are constantly being crossed in the normal process of living, but the word invasion is used as an unwelcome intrusion. Life is full of painful partings and disruptions, so it can be hard to tell the difference between tough love and abuse. The tradition of *keisatsu* in Zen Buddhism uses a flat stick to hit a monk or meditator. It is usually to stop the meditator from becoming drowsy and sleepy, and is done with the permission of the student. There are stories of people being hit using *keisatsu* so it brings them deep insight.

The roots of human violence, therefore, are totally embedded in the fundamental systems principles. Violence is not an external evil that disrupts our pure state, as Rousseau might have us believe. It is woven into our being from the start and will be with us to the end.

This is not to say we can do nothing about our violent nature. You and I can reconnect back to ourselves, others, and to the environment in which we live. We can learn to better contain the disorder in our lives and build skills for resolving conflict in positive ways that are life-affirming.

The more civilised we have become in the Western world, the more we have become separated from ourselves, each other, and the world in which we live. We remain willing to use violence to resolve problems. Systems provides a new way to see ourselves that affords the possibility of reconnecting in new, wholesome ways, but it means embracing a complex world where we play our part in the tapestry of life rather than being in control. You are invited on a journey to come to know yourself in a new way and rebuild the connections that lead to a more fulfilling, productive life.

Key Points

1 Systems Theory is the science of how things connect and disconnect
2 A system is a collection of parts that connect together to create a new whole that can do things the individual parts could not do alone
3 Parts come together because they can achieve more together than apart
4 Distinctions create boundaries. We can divide something into parts in different ways
5 How we choose to divide things matters
6 Feedback loops generate complex behaviours
7 Everything in the universe winds down over time
8 Life turns chaos into order
9 Conflict is inherent in life. It is woven into the fabric of life from the beginning. We cannot eradicate it, but we can learn to manage it
10 We can define violence as the invasion of a boundary or the disruption of a flow across a boundary.

Notes

1 This analogy is from the work of Gregory Bateson.
2 See *Politics as a Vocation* by Max Weber.

3 Rocks might interact at a subatomic level, but not at the normal daily level.
4 There is no clear accepted definition of a system, but this definition suits our purposes. Even talking of parts and wholes becomes problematic because parts in a
   system are connected and not separate, and the idea of wholes without parts is
   meaningless. Arthur Koestler described a holon as something that is simultaneously both a part and a whole. Our use of systems is also different from the word
   systematic, when it means following a fixed plan.
5 See the work of Dave Snowden in *Cynefin*.
6 This section links to the work of Derek and Laura Cabrera and their model called
   DSRP (standing for Distinctions. Systems, Relationships, and Perspective), which
   they see as fundamental to all complex systems.
7 See *Thinking in Systems: A Primer* by Donella Meadows for more detail on lags.
8 See *The Evolution of Co-operation* by Robert Axelrod.
9 System archetypes were first developed by Jay Forrester and expanded by people
   like Donella Meadows and Peter Senge.
10 See *Wicked Problems* by C West Churchman.
11 This is the second law of thermodynamics. A good source of a deeper understanding of entropy and how it works in living systems is the work of Howard Odum.
12 Systems with a flow like this were named *dissipative systems* by Ilya Prigogine
   because they dissipate the energy that comes through them.
13 See *The Origin of Humanness in the Biology of Love* by Humberto Maturana.
14 See *Steps to an Ecology of Mind* by Gregory Bateson.
15 See *Principles of the Self Organising System* by W Ross Ashby.

Bibliography

Ackoff, R. L. (1989). From Data to Wisdom. *Journal of Applied Systems Analysis, 16,*
   3–9.
Ackoff, R. L. (1999). *Ackoff's Best: His Classic Writings on Management.* Wiley.
   http://www.amazon.com/Ackoffs-Best-Classic-Writings-Management/dp/
   0471316342
Ashby, W. R. (1947). Principles of the Self-Organizing Dynamic System. *The Journal
   of General Psychology, 37*(2), 125–128. https://doi.org/10.1080/00221309.1947.9
   918144
Ashby, W. R. (1957). *An Introduction to Cybernetics.* Chapman & Hall.
Ashby, W. R., & Conant, R. (1970). Every Good Regulator of a System Must Be a
   Model of That System. *International Journal of Systems Science, 1,* 511–519.
   https://api.semanticscholar.org/CorpusID:18398641
Ashby, W. R., & Conant, R. (1991). Every Good Regulator of a System must be a
   Model of that System. In *Facets of Systems Science* (no 7). Springer, International
   Series on Systems Science and Engineering.
Axelrod, R., Hamilton, W. D. D., Bagrow, J. P., Hamilton, W. D. D., Axelrod, R., &
   Hamilton, W. D. D. (1981). The Evolution of Co-operation. *Science, 211*(4489),
   1390–1396. https://doi.org/10.1126/science.7466396
Bateson, G. (1987). *Steps to an Ecology of Mind. Collected essays in Anthropology,
   Psychiatry, Evolution, and Epistemology.* University of Chicago Press. https://doi.
   org/10.2307/446833
Bateson, G. (2002). *Mind and Nature: A Necessary Unity.* Hampton Press, Inc.
Cabrera, D., & Cabrera, L. (2015). *Systems Thinking Made Simple; New Hope for
   Solving Wicked Problems.* Cabrera Research Lab.

Cabrera, D., & Colosi, L. (2008). Distinctions, Systems, Relationships, and Perspectives (DSRP): A Theory of Thinking and of Things. *Evaluation and Program Planning*, *31*(3), 311–317. https://doi.org/10.1016/j.evalprogplan.2008.04.001

Churchman, C. W. (1967). Wicked Problems. *Management Science*, *14*(4), 141–142. https://doi.org/10.1366/000370209787169876

Forrester, J. W. (2013). *Industrial Dynamics* (Reprint). Martino Fine Books. http://www.amazon.com/Industrial-Dynamics-Jay-Wright-Forrester/dp/1614275335

Kauffman, S. A. (1993). The Origins of Order: Self Organisation and Self Selection in Evolution. In *Oxford University Press*. Oxford University Press. https://global.oup.com/academic/product/the-origins-of-order-9780195079517

Kauffman, S. A. (1995). *At Home in the Universe: The Search for the Laws of Self Organisation and Complexity*. Oxford University Press Inc.

Kauffman, S. A. (2008). *Reinventing the Sacred: A New View of Science, Reason, and Religion*. Basic Books. http://www.amazon.com/Reinventing-Sacred-Science-Reason-Religion/dp/0465003001

Luhmann, N. (1995). *Social Systems*. Stanford University Press. http://books.google.com/books?hl=en&lr=&id=zVZQW4gxXk4C&pgis=1

Maturana, H. (2002). Autopoiesis, Structural Coupling and Cognition: A History of these and other Notions in the Biology of Cognition. *Cybernetics and Human Knowing*, *9*(3), 5–34.

Maturana, H., & Varela, F. J. (1998). *The Tree of Knowledge*. Shambhala Publications.

Maturana, H., & Verden-Zoller, G. (2008). *The Origin of Humanness in the Biology of Love*. Imprint Academic.

Meadows, D. H. (2008). *Thinking in Systems* (D. Wright & C. Labrie, Eds.). Chelsea Green Publishing Company.

Meadows, D. H., Meadows, D. L., Randers, J., & Behrends III, W. (1972). *The Limits to Growth: A Report for the Club of Rome's Project on the Predicament of Mankind*. Potomac Associates.

Meadows, D. H., Randers, J., & Meadows, D. L. (2004). *Limits to Growth: The 30-Year Update*. Chelsea Green Publishing. http://www.amazon.com/Limits-Growth-The-30-Year-Update/dp/193149858X

Odum, H. (2007). *Environment, Power, and Society for the Twenty-First Century: The Hierarchy of Energy*. Columbia University Press. https://www.amazon.com/Environment-Power-Society-Twenty-First-Century-ebook/dp/B007ZDECSG/ref=sr_1_3?dchild=1&keywords=howard+odum&qid=1632305340&sr=8-3

Prigogine, I., & Stenger, I. (1984). *Order out of Chaos*. New Science Library.

Senge, P. M. (2006). *The Fifth Discipline, The Art & Practice of the Learning Organization*. Doubleday.

Snowden, D., Goh, Z., Borchardt, S., Greenberg, R., Bertsch, B., & Blignaut, S. (2020). *Cynefin - Weaving Sense-Making into the Fabric of Our World* (Kindle). Cognitive Edge Pte. https://www.amazon.com/Cynefin-Weaving-Sense-Making-Fabric-World-ebook/dp/B08LZKDCYM/ref=sr_1_1?keywords=david+snowden&qid=1637034923&s=books&sr=1-1

Weber, M. (1972). *Politics as a Vocation*. Fortress Press. http://www.amazon.com/Politics-vocation-Facet-books-Social/dp/B0006RJAXU

Chapter 2

Living Systems

Introduction

Having covered the foundational concepts that shape the way complex adaptive systems operate, the next two chapters move on to investigate living systems and their nature. They provide the background for the *Dynamics of Life* model that will be used as a blueprint to describe each level of life from a single cell to a whole human being, from a family group to nations negotiating and interacting at an international level.

All living systems create and maintain a boundaries within which energy, matter, and information is absorbed from the outside environment to overcome the disorder that would otherwise cause the living system to deteriorate and eventually die. Energy, matter, and information that cannot be used to sustain the living system is expelled back into the environment. The living system stays the same by continuously producing itself over and over.[1] These next seemingly unrelated concepts will later come together within the Dynamics of Life model. We may seem to be drifting from our main topic, but the model presented later integrates all these concepts and principles.[2]

Free Energy

Howard Odum states that living systems operate to make the most of the free energy available to them.[3] Not all energy that flows through a system is available for use. Some of it is dissipated in various ways. Very often, machines lose energy as heat.

Large amounts of sunlight provide the energy that plants capture through photosynthesis. Animals then eat the plants. Much of the energy in the plants is lost, but what is collected is more concentrated and usable than sunlight. A human being might then eat the animal or a plant to capture even more concentrated energy in order to power muscles and a brain. The energy needed to keep a human alive is only 1/10,000th of the total energy from the sun as it is processed through the food chain. It therefore takes a large area of land

DOI: 10.4324/9781003533641-2

to produce the plants to support a population of smaller animals, which are fed on by an even smaller population of predators.

Human beings tap other sources of energy, such as animal power, oil, and coal, which all originally came from the sun, and now renewable sources like wind, water, and electricity to increase our effectiveness. We can travel the globe, send rockets to the Moon and beyond, shift heavy loads, and run the global internet.

Energy flowing through a system is processed. That which cannot be processed is passed on or leaks back into the system. When we "pass the buck", there is a responsibility we do not want to get stuck with, so we hand it on to someone else to avoid the consequences. The children's game, "Hot Potato", has a small object passed around a circle while music plays. If you are holding the hot potato when the music stops playing you are eliminated from the game, and thus the hot potato gets passed around as quickly as possible. The game continues until there is only one contestant left, and this person wins a prize. Unprocessed energy, matter, and information is quickly projected away from the system, so it does not overwhelm or even kill the creature. Intense emotion that is too much for one person is often projected onto another.

If I fail to clean my room, it eventually becomes uninhabitable. Ignoring the rattle in the car engine will ultimately lead to an expensive repair bill. Excess alcohol the body cannot process slowly kills the drinker. Dumping my anger on someone unable to fight back may feel good, but it brings consequences. If I do not mow my lawns, another family member must mow them instead. A company that secretly polluted a river poisons inhabitants further downstream. If I cannot pass it on, I suffer the consequences, but passing the hot potato ends in scapegoating, with others paying the price of our unprocessed entropy. How might you recognise passing the hot potato in your life?

Fractal Energy Flows

One common problem for living systems is how to move matter, energy, or information efficiently and smoothly from a single source to a widely distributed area as in the air, entering our mouth to be dispersed evenly across the lungs. Alternatively, in the opposite direction, a flow must be gathered from a widely distributed source into one source as in rainfall being collected in a valley to become a river flowing to the sea. The most efficient way in either case turns out to be using *fractals*.[4]

A fractal is a pattern where the basic shape is repeated over and over at different scales within the fractal. Figure 2.1 shows a computer-generated fractal fern. Within this fern, you will see smaller fern shapes and, within those, even smaller reproductions of the same pattern. You notice that the scale between each level either increases or decreases by the same ratio. The first branch of a tree as in Figure 2.2 may be 50% of the trunk size. At the next branching, it is 50% the size of the previous branch, thus reducing by

Figure 2.1 A mathematically generated fractal of a fern leaf.   Barnsley Fern, Laug, https://es.m.wikipedia.org/wiki/Archivo:Barnsley_fern_2000x2000.png Creative Commons Attribution-Share Alike 4.0 International, no adaptions.

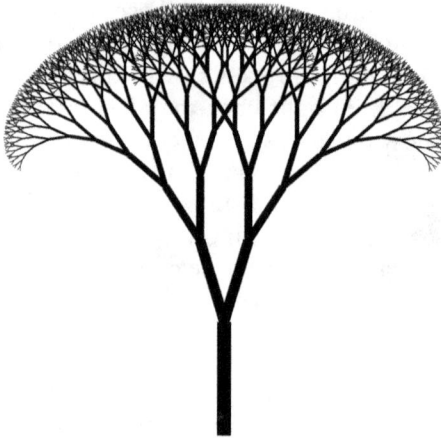

Figure 2.2 A mathematically generated fractal tree. In real-life trees, changes in conditions from year to year create irregularities.   Fractal Tree, Claudio Rocchini   https://commons.wikimedia.org/wiki/File:Fractal_canopy.svg, CC Attribution Share Alike 3.0 Unported.

50% at each branching, right down to tiny twigs that still have the basic shape of the whole tree. In nature, of course, trees face changes in growth over time, so they don't grow perfectly evenly but appear as we see them in reality.

A telephone tree works best as a fractal. The person at the top contacts, say, five people, who each contacts five, who contacts another five, who contacts another five. Already 625 people have been contacted. If we changed

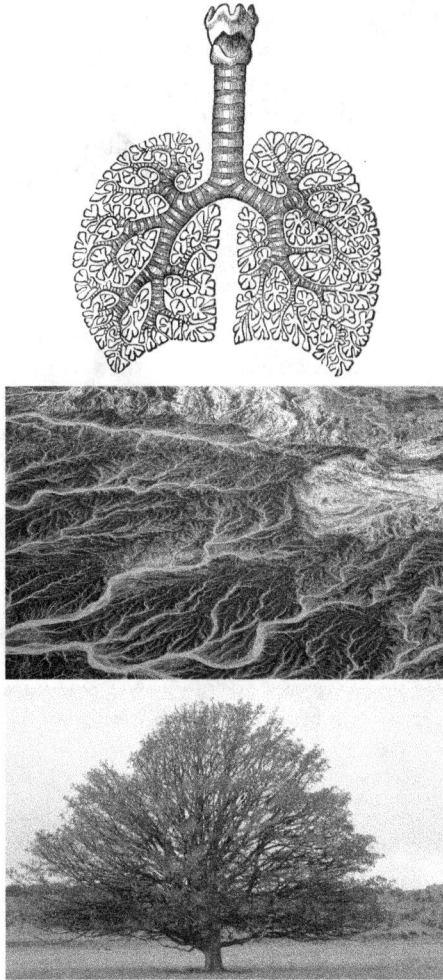

Figure 2.3 Fractal patterns in a human lung, a river valley, and a tree. Lungs iStock.com/THE PALMER; Fractal River Valley iStock.com/Wafue; Fractal tree author's photograph.

the ratio at each level, so the first level contacts 25 people each, who contacts three, who contacts 10, you can easily see blockages and delays occur that would be less effective. Nature uses fractals because they allow energy to be transferred efficiently and smoothly. Blood vessels, broccoli, and even our transport and internet systems are fractal, with equal ratios between levels. Look about you, and you will see fractals everywhere, often in places you would not imagine (Figure 2.3).

Per Bak worked with sandpiles.[5] If you drop sand on a sandpile it will lead to landslides of sand. If you measure the size of the slips, you find they fit a fractal pattern. There is a small number of big slips, a medium number of medium, slips, and a large number of smaller slips. You cannot predict what size the next slip will be; overall, however, there is a pattern. Earthquakes, deaths in wars, web pages on the internet, the size of cities, and how many sexual partners people have in their lives are all examples of such patterns. These are called Power Law Distributions. Pareto's Law, discussed in the next chapter, is also an example.

Hierarchies

Living systems form nested hierarchies. That means the parts in the living system are living systems in themselves, and the living system is a part of a bigger living system, as shown in the shape of the fern in Figure 2.4. This means a living system is typically a *system of systems*. This is rather like the Russian dolls that fit inside one another. In the human body, we have cells that interact to form tissue, that form into glands, that form into organs, that form into body systems, that come together to form a whole human being. Then people come together to form families, communities, and nations. The levels are linked fractally to facilitate effective flows of energy, matter, and information as seen in Figure 2.4.

Stafford Beer wrote about viable systems, which include living systems and organisations. His Viable Systems Model (VSM) was based originally on the systems of systems within the human body but proved to be far more widely

Figure 2.4 Living systems are typically comprised of subsystems and the system is a subsystem of a larger system.

applicable. He proposed that each viable system contains five subsystems which were themselves viable systems, that is, systems of systems. System 1 does the job of the system. In the body, it would be our heart, lungs, liver, etc. In a company, it is the factory floor. System 2 coordinates all the System 1s and provides for their needs. System 3 monitors and guides System 1 as a supervisor or bodily feedback loop. System 4 faces out into the world, providing information like sensory information or market trends for system 3 to implement. System 4 also redesigns the whole system's structure and processes to remain adaptable. System 5 has a wide overview, setting the vision and policy for the other systems to implement. System 5 has a longer-term view and needs feedback from all the systems to do its job. Figure 2.5 shows how the subsystems fit together.

Sense, Make-sense, and Respond

For a complex adaptive system to survive it must *sense, make-sense, and respond* to its environment. It must sense the relevant information about itself and the world in which it exists. Then it must discern relevant patterns to make sense of what has been perceived, allowing it to predict likely future outcomes. Finally, it formulates an appropriate response that aligns with its purpose.

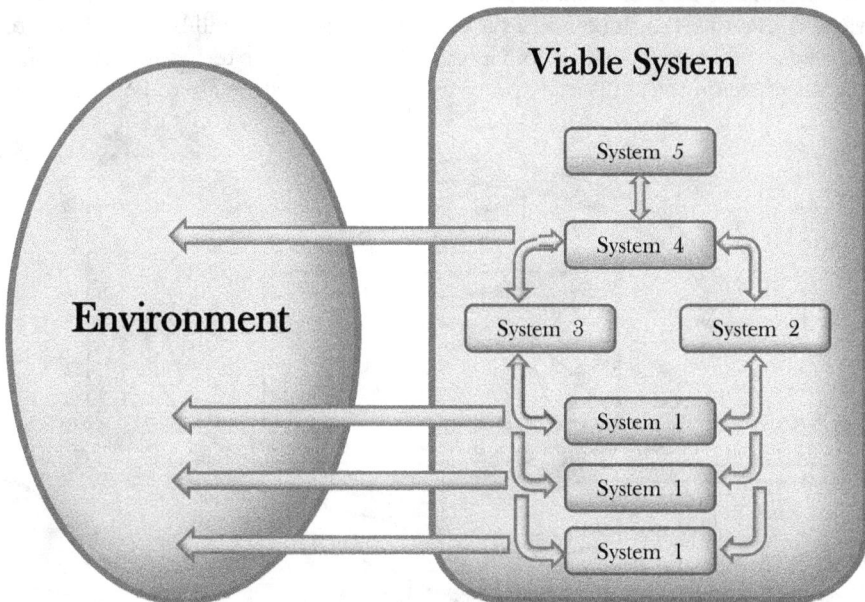

Figure 2.5 The Viable Systems Model (VSM) with Systems 1 to 5.   Reprinted with permission from the Malik Group. The author's diagram and explanation are his own and may differ from those of the Malik Group.

Living systems must monitor all their internal processes to ensure that all the processes remain within acceptable limits and fit with the needs of all the other parts. If one part goes beyond its limits, the other parts respond to bring it back within acceptable limits.

The same is true for the outside world. Again, the relevant energy, matter, and information collected must be processed and made sense of, recognising the patterns to reveal the meaning as knowledge that enables action to be selected in line with its purpose. It does this by changing its body to exert force on the world or change the body's orientation or position in ways it deems as in its best interests. This is depicted in Figure 2.6.

The inside world and the outside world both call on body energy, so a living system must balance how it uses its energy. It is like fighting a battle on two fronts. A general must decide how many troops to send to each front. The inner needs and outer needs must be managed simultaneously. It is worth looking more closely at each step in sensing, making sense, and responding.

We use our senses to gather data to metabolise, in just the same way as we metabolise food. Data is just numbers or symbols that have no meaning in themselves. When we find patterns in the data, we have information. If we have a regular flow of unchanging data like a clock ticking, it conveys no new information. When that data is represented on the clock face, it becomes information. It becomes knowledge when we can do something with it, like know it is time to get out of bed. Wisdom is being able to use the knowledge in effective ways. A creature that metabolises information effectively will be more likely to succeed at what they wish to do. George Mobus[6] uses the term sapience, which focuses more on the skills and abilities we need to accumulate to become wise.

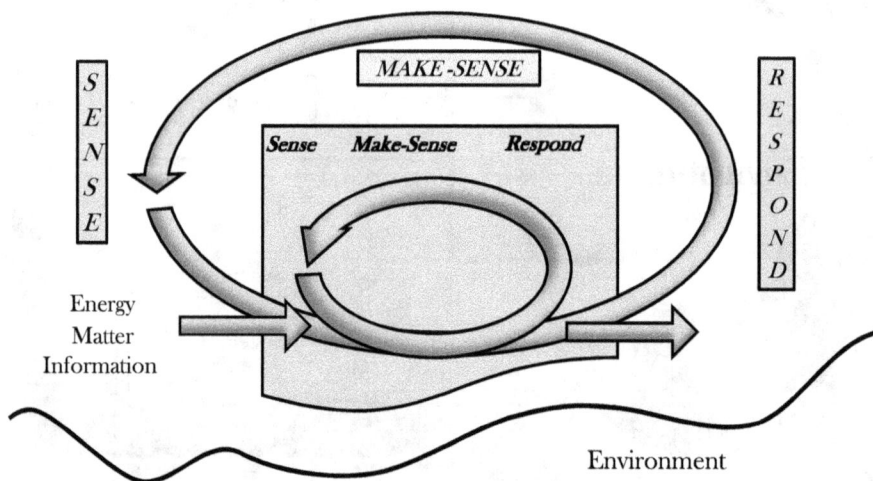

Figure 2.6 A living system must sense, make-sense, and respond to its own body; and sense, make-sense, and respond to its outside environment.

Sense

Living systems have sense organs all through the body, constantly gathering information about its internal state. The body has many functions to be regulated within critical limits, or it will lose stability. If blood pressure is allowed to rise too high, other body functions cannot operate properly. The data collected must be sufficient to monitor all critical tasks. In minded creatures, the sensory data is coded into electrical or chemical signals.

Sense organs cover the boundary with the external world to sense the state of the world, alerting the creature to threats and opportunities. When two people hug, millions of sensory cells are activated in each body in a to and fro "dance" of mutual, recursive interconnectedness.

Nora Bateson,[7] daughter of the systems pioneer Gregory Bateson,[8] writes of warm data, which sees any situation in its context as it relates to everything else rather than just objective scientific data. She gives the example of a doctor on a house visit to diagnose her mother's illness. The doctor was also noticing who was in the house, the levels of tidiness and hygiene, the atmosphere, and so much more that allowed the doctor to put the illness into context that would greatly enhance their ability to understand where the illness might have come from, and what might help or hinder the healing process.

Since a system is always less complex than the world in which it lives,[9] it can never have perfect knowledge. It must select what is most relevant. First, it only has access to information that the various sense organs can generate.[10] Dogs hear different sounds from us; bees see different colours. Colour-blind people see different colours from the rest of us. Even men and women see colours differently. In other worlds, our capabilities are bounded by the capacities of our bodies.

We measure our world against our body and its capabilities. We sense the world relative to our size and orientation. We measure our world through our hands by grasping, while a dog measures its world by how it can bite or hold something in its mouth.[11]

If we want to understand something new, we grasp it and move it around in our hands. We feel the shape, texture, colour, and temperature and look at it from different angles. We always want to reach out and touch objects because that is how we bring things into our world. We need to know what it is, how we might use it, or recognise it as an opportunity or threat. Just as we grasp and grapple with our hands, we grapple with ideas and concepts getting their feel and taking different perspectives until we grasp them.

We orient ourselves to our world to best appreciate what is happening. If you visit an art museum, you find yourself naturally standing at a certain distance from an artwork. If you move in too close, you gain a better understanding of the detail but lose the overall sense of the picture. If you stand too far away, you gain the overview but lose the detail. There is an optimum distance at which you perceive the best of both. Thus, when we come across any object, it seems to suggest a way to interact with it. A doorknob is at about hand height. It is shaped to suggest that it could be easily gripped and turned. James Gibson called such things "affordances"[12] because the door affords being opened. Affordances are all about us. In nature, rocks of the right size suggest being picked up to explore possible uses. Similarly, we design and shape objects like hammers and screwdrivers as convenient objects to use.

Secondly, the sensory information may be ambiguous. Optical illusions show how we organise data based on what we expect even before we make-sense of it. Often things can be interpreted in two or more ways, such as in the case of Wittgenstein's duck-rabbit shown in Figure 2.7. It could be a rabbit or a duck depending on how we see it. We make-sense as we sense, so we can better choose what to sense. We look closer at an object to get a better look or tilt our heads to hear a sound better.

You will also notice the duck-rabbit is just black lines on a white background, but from it you recognise the image of a rabbit and a duck. Determining whether a shape in front of us is just a rock or a grizzly bear may be a life-or-death distinction. When meaning-making is unsure, we direct our attention towards more relevant information. We orient and look closely at the rock.

Thirdly, we have limited energy for our life processes. Just as we must manage our finances economically, living systems must be economical with their energy. This is called *bio-economics* or *body budget*.[13] We do not have the time or energy to process everything we sense, so we must select what is most relevant. We create a foreground and a background. As we focus on the foreground, we defocus the background. While it saves energy, it opens the door to error.

The role of the human brain is not to create an accurate representation of the world. It is to create an experience that best enhances our ability to cope, survive, and thrive. The brain makes many assumptions to reduce energy that are true often enough to be worth the cost of occasional errors.

Figure 2.7 Wittgenstein's rabbit-duck. This picture can be either a duck looking to the left or a rabbit looking to the right.   CPA Media Pte Ltd/Alamy Stock Photo. Photo by Pictures From History.

Fourthly, the brain creates our experience from the information it has selected. We perceive the world as existing in a three-dimensional space, but the data entering our two eyes creates two two-dimensional images. The brain weaves it all into one experience. Our experiences are constructed from the data gleaned, rather than reflecting the world out there as it is. Since the core purpose of life is maintaining life, it is more important that we have an experience that enables us to sense, make-sense, and respond effectively than it is for the brain to create an exact experience of the world.

Our brains must work in real time. When a ball is thrown at us, the time it takes for the brain to process the image is long enough for the ball to have moved. We actually see the ball where the brain thinks it will be at the time we perceive it, or we cannot catch it. We do not see what is there, we see what works.

Make-Sense

Just as we metabolise food to acquire the energy to act, we metabolise information gathered by the senses in order to know what to do. Data is processed to extract meaning that tells us what to do. The core of making-sense is recognising patterns because they reduce the complexity to be processed. If I see six things that are the same, when I understand one, I understand the other five. Most usually patterns continue into the future, allowing us to make predictions about future situations. The sun has always risen in the morning. It is a reasonable expectation that it will do so tomorrow. Waves move across the ocean in predictable ways that can tell us about the past. The wake of a ship not only tells us a ship recently passed, but also how big it is and in what direction it travelled. There are longer-term patterns like a life cycle from a baby to a child to an adolescent to an adult to old age and death. We connect patterns with other patterns to form a coherent network of patterns that map us and the world we live in. The map guides us, so we know what to do. When we have made sense of a situation, we can choose what information we should focus on.

Responding

We use our body to respond to the world. We change its shape and configuration to exert force on the environment to make changes. We are also creatures of the future because everything we do changes our bodies to be ready for anticipated future events. There are always limits on our body's capacity to respond. We might lack physical strength or cognitive capacity for certain tasks. We might have an injury or an illness that restricts our actions. As we age, our body wears down.

The Three Steps Together

Sensing, making sense, and responding were presented above as three steps, but all three steps occur simultaneously all the time. As I sense I make-sense, so I know what to focus on. As I make-sense I keep sensing, orienting my body to gain better information. As I respond I sense my response, so I gain useful feedback. As I reach for my coffee cup, I sense where my hand is and where the cup is, make-sense of the relationship between the two, so I can move to grasp it.

Cognition is usually equated to the making sense part of sensing, making sense, and responding. As we see, however, all three of these processes are inextricably entangled. Cognition does not just happen in the front part of the brain as is usually presented; rather, it requires the whole brain. More than that, cognition requires a body to act in the world and the body has no meaning without an environment in which it lives. Even the coffee cup I reach towards is a part of my cognition; sensing, making sense, and responding so I can act in the world.

The art of mindfulness is a powerful way of building awareness of sensing, making sense, and responding. Stop and notice what you sense, the sights, the smells, the sounds, the tastes, and more. Notice the emotions as they arise or the thoughts that arise from your belief systems. Notice your urge to respond to what is felt, either because it is uncomfortable, or because it is comfortable and pleasant. There is value in learning to cope better and become more comfortable accepting uncomfortable feelings, so you are freer to act proactively. You can build the skill of being present in the moment by practicing awareness as you sense, make-sense, and respond. The most ordinary of activities like gardening, walking, cleaning, and waiting for traffic lights are all opportunities to practice mindfulness.

Identity and the Will to Live

Identity is that which is conserved in the process of living. Living systems work to preserve their identity, which is expressed as a will to live. This includes protecting what is unique. Living systems have hidden or private parts to maintain their integrity and avoid becoming overrun by external influences. We have private parts of our body. There are state secrets and there is commercially sensitive information. The parts that make us up also have their own identity. We have suppressed emotions that we hide from ourselves.

We develop a sense of identity as a map of ourselves to be conserved. Sooner or later, life events will challenge the map. Changing the map is bio-economically expensive. When we find ourselves lacking in some way, it is often easier to blame others or to create stories to justify ourselves than it is to restructure our identity. We then maintain our existing identity by distorting how we see the world rather than changing our internal cognitive map.

We do not respond to other people as they are, but rather according to the identity we have created in our minds as to who we think they are. What are the parts of your identity that best define you? How do you protect this identity and how do you respond when it is challenged?

The Other

Whenever a part or a system is defined, an *other* beyond the boundary of the part or the system is simultaneously brought into existence.[14] Shining a light creates a shadow. A system always exists in an environment, so the environment is a part of the other. What is included within the system, such as other group members, is more familiar and trusted. We have a strong urge to trust the familiar. What is outside the system is less familiar, so there is a suspicion of the outsider deep within our being. We often see ourselves as right, making the other wrong. The other easily becomes the enemy. It is also easy to depict ourselves as the victim of the other, leading to self-justifications to attack the other.

Supersystems of which the system is a part and subsystems within the system have their own boundaries and identity, so they all have their own conception of the other. Often the other of our subsystems remain within us. An overactive gland produces chemicals that harm the body, a rebellious worker sows discord in a factory, and a suppressed emotion festers inside. That which we reject has lessons to teach us and will keep returning until we discover how to connect, manage, and make peace with our other.

The Power to Act

Autonomous living systems have the power to act in the world by organising the energy flow through them.[15] As we make choices, we constrain and direct our energy towards certain goals. Nothing can act without power, but power can be used for either good or bad.

The whole of civilisation rests on people ceding power to others to act in ways they hope will be of mutual benefit. Sometimes we ceded that authority willingly; at other times, it is forced upon us. We are born into a world where agreements made by other people remain binding on us. A teacher has the power to tell a student what to do so that they learn. A child may need to go to a hospital for treatment. The child may not want to go because they know the injection will be painful and yet the parent must have the right to take the child to the hospital even though it is against the child's wishes. We have laws we must obey. We can choose to disobey, but there will be consequences. It is not power over people as such that is the problem, it is the way power over people is used.

The edge between using power to teach a tough life lesson and harming someone is often not as sharply defined as we might like. We might think we are being supportive when we cause harm. In many ways, the challenge of this book is how to find ways to work with power that enhances life rather than destroys it.

Rule Sets

Rule sets govern all living systems. They constrain the activities of the parts to ensure that their actions fit within the bounds that maintain the cohesion of the whole living system. The parts cannot act as they wish. They must coordinate their efforts. Terence Deacon[16] writes of this as an absence because of lost possibilities for the parts. Alicia Juarrero writes of enabling constraints. When we can do anything, we can do nothing until we make a choice. It is only when we add constraints that we create possibilities. If I want to go on a holiday to Spain, I block out the options of going to England or buying a car.

Simpler forms of life are controlled by rules embedded in DNA molecules that act as algorithms determining the living system's actions. A single-celled paramecium has a rule that if it notices a reduction in the concentration of glucose on which it feeds, it randomly turns in another direction, thereby increasing its chances of finding more glucose. People have rule sets based on belief systems and nations have constitutions and laws.

The absorbed energy, matter, and information is acted on according to the rule set. The parts of the system need to adhere to the rules sufficiently in order to maintain the integrity and cohesion of the whole system. There will always be some defecting from the rule set, but as long as that is not too forceful, the system will cope. The police do not catch all criminals, but if they catch enough, society still functions well.

Since the parts of a system are also autonomous units, they have their own rule sets. Sometimes the rule sets at various levels clash. What I want for myself might clash with the needs of my family or my community. My desire for chocolate cake may clash with my need to balance blood sugar levels. The clash of rule sets in a hierarchy is a common cause of conflict and violence.

There must be ways to reward compliance with the rule set and punish or discourage defections from the rule set. At the physical level, the brain creates sensations of pleasure or pain to alert the creature to the consequences of actions. On a societal level, we reward people through awards and social approval and enforce the rule set through the police and other authorities.

At the physical level, the body is the manifestation of the rule set. The body is shaped by the environment in which it lives, becoming a mapping of the world it lives in. Natural selection homes in on body shapes, sizes, and colours that increase fitness because those who are not fit do not survive. Camouflage is an excellent example. In this way, the qualities of the world are imprinted in the body itself. If the world changes, the body must adapt.

Creatures that only have a body and no centralised brain can still cognise and function surprisingly well at a lower level of consciousness. Sponges, starfish, sea cucumbers, and other sea creatures have no brain. An octopus has a small, centralised brain. Each leg of an octopus can operate independently, but they co-ordinate their actions, allowing the octopus to act as one coherent organism. An octopus can escape from a tank to eat other fish and crabs and return to their tank. They can open jars, make tools, and escape through a coin-sized hole. Such creatures have body wisdom. We too have a highly developed sense of body wisdom that often gets lost under all our brain activity. Body wisdom is a critical part of our day-to-day functioning.

We use a physical map to find where we are in relation to the territory in which we stand. We find where we are on our map and then plot a course to reach our desired destination. The more accurate the map, the more likely it is to lead us in the right direction. The mapping imprinted in our bodies and minds as a result of our previous interactions guides our actions in the world. Our mental map lets us know where we are, and what we need to do to achieve our goals. If our mental and physical mapping has significant errors, our behaviour will become maladaptive. What are all the rule sets you must manage: your family, your city, your nation, your church, your culture? What happens when they clash? How are the rules enforced or rewarded?

Memory

Living systems must store energy, matter, and information to be retrieved when needed later. Memory is stored information, or knowledge, that allows the recognition of patterns and thus predictions of likely futures. Information is encoded in the DNA molecule. Humans accumulate knowledge and wisdom that is handed from generation to generation. Writing made that much easier and now with digital storage we all have access to enormous amounts of information to enrich our lives. It requires energy to maintain memory and is prone to error since it degrades over time.

Values

Whatever helps sustain survival is attributed a positive value and whatever threatens well-being has a negative value. Values become enshrined in the rule set. Animals came to value light over dark, front over back, warm over cold, open over closed, visible over hidden, and higher over lower because they increase safety. We also came to value right over left. The general preference for the right-hand side may have been a quirk of evolution that became embedded in the DNA or arose because the left brain controlling the right side of the body controls detailed precise actions that would be helpful if under attack. This preference for the right is embedded in languages. The Latin for right is *dexter* and the Latin for left is *sinister*. Similarly, in French right is *droit* (adroit) and left is *gauche*. The right has become valued over the left.

A metaphor is formed when one thing is linked to something else.[17] Linking light with safety is a metaphor. Dark is linked to threat, harm, and pain. We are wired for safety. Even wild animals have a metaphorical mapping of their world that they use to survive and thrive.

Resisting Change

Change involves risk and rewiring the mapping is expensive bio-economically, so living systems resist change. Perhaps the old response is not optimal, but a new response could be fatal. Often it is a case of "Better the devil you know" or "If it ain't broke, don't fix it". Life typically resists change until there is no further option. Our sense of identity is strongly tied to our mental map of who we are and how we fit into the world. A threat to our map feels like a threat to life itself. Rather than go through the painful restructuring of our mental model, we may blame, project, justify, or deny the reality of the world. This allows us to maintain our existing mental map. Notice situations where you resist change. Where does the resistance come from? How would it be to accept the change?

Curiosity

There is opportunity in the unknown. A creature that braves the unknown and succeeds will have an advantage over a similar creature that stays within its known limits. If we do not take reasonable risks to explore the unknown, we will be left behind compared to those who take a reasonable risk. We do not stop crossing the road because there is a small possibility we could get hit by a car.

When we do not understand our situation, we become extremely uncomfortable. We must explore so that we know. We spent millions of dollars trying to find Malaysia Airlines flight MH370 when it mysteriously went missing over the Indian Ocean. Detectives solve crimes, so we know what happened. When we know, we feel safe and able to embrace the future.

Trade-offs

Life is full of trade-offs. Birds have wings to fly, but in gaining flight they forfeit other uses of the limbs. Making one part of a system more effective frequently makes another less effective. If I design a house with fixed external walls, making one room bigger means another becomes smaller.

We already explored the trade-offs between chaos and order, and autonomy and connectivity. Life is about finding the sweet spot between the two, where the dynamic balance is just right. John Vervaeke calls this opponent processing. The simple act of running can only occur because we repeat a dynamic pattern of coordinated movements between our two legs. If we freeze at any moment, we fall.

Living systems have three critical constraints that impact how they function in the world. These are speed, accuracy, and energy. They must be able to respond in time before the situation becomes critical or the opportunity is lost. They must choose a sufficiently accurate response that meets the challenge using the least energy possible. The brain is only 2% of the body by weight but consumes 20% or more of the available energy. It wants to get the "biggest bang for its buck".

A more accurate response takes longer to formulate and uses more energy. A quick response uses less energy, but is likely to lead to an error of judgment. We must somehow decide when we have gathered enough information to act.

We seek the "good enough" response[18] to meet the needs of the moment. You may have seen a long-distance truck driver hitting the tyres with a stick. He needs a measure of the tyre pressure. The sound the tyre makes when hit by the stick does not measure the exact tyre pressure, but the sound the driver hears provides an adequate quick and easy indication. A baseball player catching a ball cannot compute all the angles and velocities to be in the right place to catch the ball, but if they keep the ball on a linear path at a constant 45-degree angle as they run, they can reach the place where the ball will land.

The brain uses many assumptions that are usually true to reduce energy consumption. The more we can assume to be true, the less we need to evaluate. We generally assume the car in front of us indicating a left turn, will actually turn left. The problem is that sometimes our assumptions are incorrect and there may be a cost. We may crash into the car ahead. As long as the cost incurred by occasional false assumptions is low enough, the assumption is still the optimal strategy.

Optical illusions arise because the brain makes an incorrect assumption about what it perceives. When we see two lines converging towards a point at the top, as in the Ponzo illusion in Figure 2.8, most often it is because two parallel lines are receding into the distance as in railway lines or lines of trees on the roadside. The brain assumes it is viewing a three-dimensional image of railway tracks, so the top arrow appears further away than the bottom arrow. To make sense of this contradiction, the brain makes the top arrow appear longer than it is, but if you measure them, you will see they are the same.

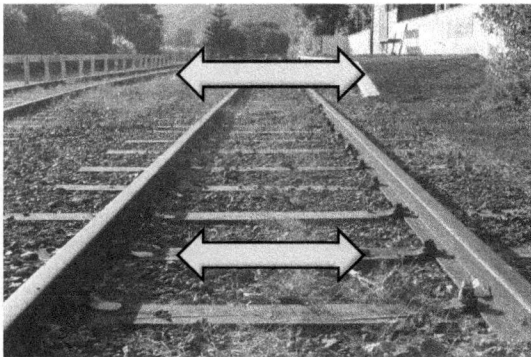

Figure 2.8 The Ponzo illusion.   Author's photograph.

Gregg Henriques describes creatures weighing up the cost of achieving a goal against the cost of failure.[19] That needs to include a risk assessment. He cites a water buffalo walking towards the water with the risk of a crocodile lurking beneath the surface. It approaches cautiously ready to bolt if anything feels unsafe. Humans can be seen weighing up the gains of winning an altercation against the implications of losing a fight or loss of social reputation. They might consider the gain from stealing against the risk and the implications of getting caught.

Key Points

1 Life exists by forming a boundary that takes in a flow of energy, matter, and information to sustain itself.
2 Any disorder that cannot be processed by a system is passed on to others or leaks toxically into itself.
3 Nature uses fractal formations as it is the most efficient way of moving energy, matter, or information through a system.
4 Living systems typically form systems of systems like Russian dolls. The parts of a living system are themselves parts and the living system is a part of a bigger living system.
5 All life must sense, make-sense, and respond inside its body and in its environment.
6 All living systems have a unique identity. Defining an identity simultaneously defines the "other".
7 Rule sets determine the actions of parts within systems to carry out the necessary functions. If there is insufficient compliance the well-being of the system may be impacted.
8 All living systems have values that guide their actions.
9 Life resists change.
10 Life arises out of trade-offs such as autonomy and connectivity.
11 Living creatures must act with sufficient speed, and accuracy and use the least reasonable energy. They seek a good enough response.

Notes

1 Maturana calls this process autopoiesis, from the Greek *auto* meaning self and *poiesis* meaning producing.
2 Also useful for an overview of living systems is the work of Fritjof Capra.
3 See *Environment, Power, and Society* by Howard Odum.
4 See *The Fractal Geometry of Nature*. by Benoit Mandelbrot, who pioneered the understanding of fractals by revealing their mathematical structure.
5 See *How Nature Works: The Science of Self-Organized Criticality* by Per Bak.
6 See *A Theory of Sapience: Using Systems Science to Understand the Nature of Wisdom and the Human Mind* by George Mobus.
7 See *Small Arcs of Wider Circles Framing through Other Patterns* by Nora Bateson.

8 See *Ecology of Minds* and *Mind and Nature: A Necessary Unity* by Gregory Bateson.
9 See *Social Systems* by Niklas Luhmann.
10 Maturana and Varela call this *structural determinism*, where a creature's capacities are determined by the body and its capacities.
11 See *Phenomenology of Perception* by Maurice Merleau Ponty.
12 See *The Ecological Approach to Visual Perception* by James Gibson.
13 See *How Emotions are Made: The Secret Life of the Brain* by Lisa Feldman Barrett.
14 See *The Theory and Practice of Boundary Critique* by Midgley, Munlo, & Brown.
15 See *The Will to Power* by Friedrich Nietzsche.
16 See *Incomplete Nature: How Mind Emerges from Matter* by Terrence Deacon.
17 See *Metaphors We Live By* by George Lakoff and Mark Johnson.
18 See http://asc-cybernetics.org/2004/glanvillepaper.pdf by Ranulph Glanville.
19 See *A New Unified Theory of Psychology* Gregg Henriques for information on his Behaviour Investment Theory.

Bibliography

Bak, P. (1996). *How Nature Works: The Science of Self Organized Criticality.* Copernicus, an imprint of Springer-Verlag.
Barnsley, M. (2013). *Fractals Everywhere* (New Edition). Dover Publications.
Bateson, G. (1987). *Steps to an Ecology of Mind. Collected Essays in Anthropology, Psychiatry, Evolution, and Epistemology.* University of Chicago Press. https://doi.org/10.2307/446833
Bateson, G. (2002). *Mind and Nature: A Necessary Unity.* Hampton Press, Inc.
Bateson, N. (2016). *Small Arcs of Larger Circles Framing through Other Patterns.* Triarchy Press.
Beer, S. (1984). The Viable System Model: Its Provenance, Development, Methodology and Pathology. *Journal of the Operational Research Society*, 35(1), 7–25. https://doi.org/10.2307/2581927
Capra, F. (1997). *The Web of Life: A New Scientific Understanding of Living Systems.* Anchor. http://www.amazon.com/The-Web-Life-Scientific-Understanding/dp/0385476760
Capra, F., & Luisi, P. L. (2014). *The Systems View of Life: A Unifying Vision.* Cambridge University Press.
Deacon, T. (2011). *Incomplete Nature: How Mind Emerged from Matter* (1st Edition). W. W. Norton and Co. https://www.amazon.com/Incomplete-Nature-Mind-Emerged-Matter-ebook/dp/B005LW5JAS/ref=sr_1_2?crid=2CSIGBFK9QKUS&dib=eyJ2IjoiMSJ9.3eCXjMdmO0lRhHV6Kao3uBrypx77LvQBrBe8unTUpduXomfKSd4AxJRpoZb9ryeBHrU3mv6KiQWmAwdr8_6zovt8yYANhA15Hdoiv3Dae4Pv5Whdy-KFt5Y-_-FspAsebhHV9TsZ2IMCRMdYbLIJOw.zhyy6QFWPTgHGVBCBcEqIXG3xNSwO0nqsojSPpG979w&dib_tag=se&keywords=terence+deacon&qid=1719140874&s=books&sprefix=terrence+deacon%2Cstripbooks-intl-ship%2C405&sr=1-2
Espejo, R., & Harnden, R. (1990). The Viable System Model: Interpretations and Applications of Stafford Beer's VSM. *The Journal of the Operations Research Society*, 41(9), 893–894.

Feldman Barrett, L. (2017). *How Emotions are Made: The Secret Life of the Brain.* Pan Books. https://www.amazon.com/How-Emotions-Are-Made-Thinking-ebook/dp/B06WLMGNRX?ref_=ast_author_dp

Gibson, J. J. (2015). *The Ecological Approach to Visual Perception* (Classic edition). Psychology Press.

Henriques, G. (2022). *A New Synthesis for Solving the Problem of Psychology: Addressing the Enlightenment Gap.* Palgrave Macmillan. https://www.amazon.com/Synthesis-Solving-Problem-Psychology-Enlightenment-ebook/dp/B0BPQFYLTG/ref=sr_1_1?crid=2K8ZHMGHJLMH&keywords=gregg+henriques&qid=1677049032&sprefix=gregg+henriques%2Caps%2C480&sr=8-1

Juarrero, A. (2023). *Context Changes Everything: How Constraints Create Coherence.* MIT Press.

Lakoff, G. (1992). The Contemporary Theory of Metaphor. http://terpconnect.umd.edu/~israel/lakoff-ConTheorMetaphor.pdf

Lakoff, G., & Johnson, M. (1980). *Metaphors We Live By.* University of Chicago Press.

Luhmann, N. (1995). *Social Systems.* Stanford University Press. http://books.google.com/books?hl=en&lr=&id=zVZQW4gxXk4C&pgis=1

Mandelbrot, B. B. (1982). *The Fractal Geometry of Nature.* W. H. Freeman and Company. http://www.amazon.com/Fractal-Geometry-Nature-Benoit-Mandelbrot/dp/0716711869

Maturana, H. (2002). Autopoiesis, Structural Coupling and Cognition: A History of these and Other Notions in the Biology of Cognition. *Cybernetics and Human Knowing, 9*(3), 5–34.

Merleau Ponty, M. (2012). *The Phenomenology of Perception.* Routledge.

Midgley, G., Munlo, I., & Brown, M. (1998). The Theory and Practice of Boundary Critique: Developing Housing Services for Older the Theory and Practice of Boundary Critique: Developing Housing Services for Older People. *Source: The Journal of the Operational Research Society Journal of the Operational Research Society, 49*(49), 467–478. https://doi.org/10.1057/palgrave.jors.2600531

Midgley, G., & Pinzón, L. A. (2011). Boundary Critique and its Implications for Conflict Prevention. *Journal of the Operational Research Society, 62*(8), 1543–1554. https://doi.org/10.1057/jors.2010.76

Mobus, G. (2017). A Theory of Sapience: Using Systems Theory to Understand the Nature of Wisdom and the Human mind. https://mahb.stanford.edu/library-item/theory-sapience-using-systems-science-understand-nature-wisdom-human-mind/

Nietzsche, F. W., Hill, R. K., & Scarpitti, M. A. (2017). *The Will to Power: Selections from the Notebooks of the 1880s.* Penguin Classics.

Odum, H. T. (Howard T.) (2007). Environment, Power, and Society for the Twenty-First Century: The hierarchy of energy. 418. Colombia University Press.

O'Neill, R. V., & Hall, C. A. S. (1996). Maximum Power: The Ideas and Applications of H. T. Odum. *Ecology, 77*(7), 2263. https://doi.org/10.2307/2265721

Vervaeke, J. (2019). Awakening from the Meaning Crisis. YouTube Video Series. youtube.com/watch?v=5418_ewcOIY

Vervaeke, J. (2020, May). Diagnosing the Current Age: A Symptomology of the Meaning Crisis. https://thesideview.co/journal/diagnosing-the-current-age/

Vervaeke, J., Lillicrap, T., & Richards, B. (2009). Relevance Realization and the Emerging Framework in Cognitive Science. *Journal on Logic and Computation Advance Access.*

Chapter 3

Further Concepts

Introduction

This chapter extends the concepts introduced in the previous one, particularly exploring the nature of cognition, and extending it from the brain into the body and even the environment. Then, we learn about the levels of evolution we have passed through, before delving into more concepts around the systemic tensions in life. That finally prepares us for the *Dynamics of Life* model, which forms the foundation of the investigations of our human nature and how we might reconnect to realise our full potential.

Cognition

The body is the foundation of life. All autonomous living creatures have a body. Body wisdom is a direct knowing within the body about its internal state and its relationship to its environment. Cognition arises from the body. The emotional, mental, and social layers of a human being emerge out of the body and cannot exist without it. We know our emotions from the bodily sensations we experience.[1] Thinking emerges from our emotions. Thinking therefore needs a body as a foundation.

A body tells its history. If you have received a wound in the past, a record of it remains in your body as a scar. Over time, body posture will be distorted in the direction of our habitual responses to our life experiences. Depressed people may develop hunched shoulders. People with long-term aggressive natures can adopt a posture where the arms are permanently out from the body ready to fight.

We carry our ancestors with us, not only in our memory but also imprinted into our bodies. The whole history of human beings is written into our being. Our body includes single-celled bacteria. A human embryo grows through clearly observable stages in the same order as our evolutionary development. The layers of the human brain reflect the evolutionary stages of life from reptiles to mammals to humans.

DOI: 10.4324/9781003533641-3

Bodily processes have a rhythm so the various functions can be coordinated. When at rest many body functions occur at around 60 beats a minute, so music with this beat, such as much of Mozart's work, is perceived as soothing. Dance is moving the body in rhythmic patterns. Similarly, a group of people harmonising their body movements or singing together builds an alignment within the group that enhances group cohesion.

Creatures respond and adapt to other creatures and their environment interacting back and forth to the point they become entangled.[2] The boundary between them and other creatures becomes blurred. The Egyptian Plover, for example, lands in the mouth of a crocodile and eats the food stuck to the teeth. The bird gains food and the crocodile has its teeth cleaned. The crocodile could easily eat the bird, but it has learned that it gains more by not doing so. Two symbiotically linked creatures can become so interdependent that if one dies or goes away, the other cannot survive. Both animals gain from the arrangement. By contrast, a parasite gains at the expense of the host.

A conversation is a communication between two or more people, where each is constantly changing the other. Both can influence the conversation, but neither controls it. Nobody can perfectly predict how a conversation will go; it is almost as if it has a life of its own.

A system can only be fully understood within the context of its environment. It is like an actor on the stage standing in the foreground. They are the focus, but what is happening to other characters and the various props and backgrounds provide the context to understand why the actor is doing what they are doing.[3]

Anticipation

It is not enough to be aware and respond in the moment. If you walk towards a large hole in the ground, you do not wait to act until you are on the verge of falling in. You want to anticipate the future danger from far off. By predicting the likely outcome, you walk around the hole or turn back. Responding to what is happening in the present is called feedback; anticipating the future is called *feedforward*.[4] Everything we do is aimed at changing our state of being to bring about the future conditions we consider will best meet our living needs.

In the most basic forms of life, the future is anticipated through natural selection. Animals acting with ineffective responses die out, so those which survive anticipate the future and enhance their likelihood of survival. An acorn has evolved as a seed that anticipates growing into a mighty oak tree. The single-celled paramecium anticipates the future by responding to chemical changes in the environment. As creatures become more complex, the sophistication of how they anticipate the future increases.

Robert Rosen describes how we anticipate the future, as shown in Figure 3.1. We estimate likely or expected futures and act to change the futures towards

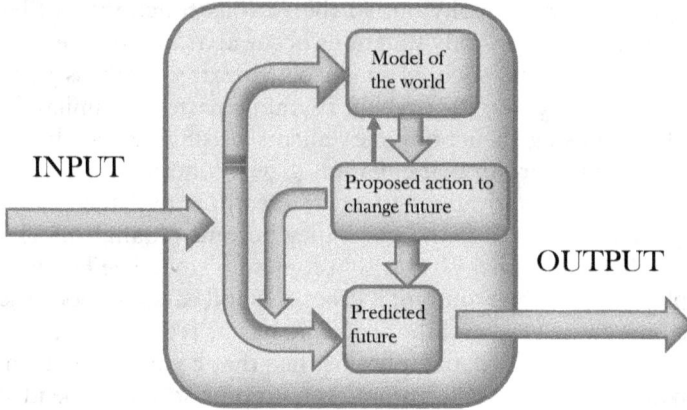

Figure 3.1 Robert Rosen's diagram of an anticipatory system. The living system has a model of itself and its world that predicts the future and then generates interventions to bring about the preferred future before the initial predicted future happens.   Reprinted with permission of Judith Rosen.

that preferred likely future before the first future happens. Every time we act, we change the future, so we must constantly re-predict likely future states and act to change them. If we like the likely future, we can work to ensure it happens.

The best predictor of what will happen in the future is generally what happened in the past. The more accurately we can predict a likely outcome, the better our decisions. We notice patterns through time or space. When I drop something heavy on my foot, it hurts, and I feel pain. When I stay up too late, I am tired the next day. When I run too fast, I fall over. Knowing these patterns helps predict consequences.

We can also make inferences from situations that are similar but not precisely the same. If I know what it feels like to have a book fall on my foot, I can extend my prediction to what might happen if a hammer falls on my foot. I might also note when a pattern ends. I anticipate the need to fill my car up with petrol before the tank runs empty or replace a fraying rope before it breaks.[5]

4e Cognition

Cognition is much more than what happens in the front of our brain. The idea of 4e cognition proposes that cognition is *Embodied*, *Embedded*, *Enacted*, and *Extended*.[6] All living organisms have a body. Organisations are comprised of people who have bodies, so life is *Embodied*. As we have seen, cognition is not confined to the front of the brain but extends through the whole body. The brain and peripheral nervous system stretching through the body are not separate. It is all one continuous nervous system from the top of our heads to our toes. We could say some of our brains are in our toes. We have significant neural networks in the stomach and gut which are larger than the brains of some creatures. These networks are all a part of human cognition. Much of the brain's messaging occurs using hormones through the endocrine system. Other systems, of course, like the circulatory system and the immune system, are also needed to support the brain's functions.

The body is the foundation of life that connects our inner being to the outer world. We can only change the world through our bodies. Every action is embodied. Our bodies evolved to function in our living environment. We have a binary structure where the left and right sides are roughly mirror images, because putting tension on symmetrical parts enables optimal forward movement through the environment and the symmetry assists in balance. There are differences such as our heart being on the left. Our brain has two halves, the left side focusing more on existing predictable situations, and the right for more creative and innovative responses to unknown needs. The two sides are connected and integrated through the nerve fibres of the corpus callosum, so the two sides act as one. The binary nature allows distinctions to be made, but the interconnectedness between complementary spaces speaks to our integrated nature.

The body is *Embedded* within an environment rather than just being a body existing in an environment. We change our world as our world changes us. We know things by grasping them. We get a handle on things. We grasp an idea and chew it over. The embeddedness of cognition has come through to our language and the metaphors that arise from the movement and relationship of our body in the world.

We say cognition is *Enactive* because cognition occurs any time we act with our body. If I want to know if a nut will fit on a bolt, I use my body to try it out. No other way will tell me for sure. Maturana says "All knowing is doing and all doing is knowing".[7] It is through responding and interacting that we come to know and learn.

Cognition is *Extended*. We use tools to extend the capabilities of our bodies. A hammer makes our arm longer and its weight means we can exert greater force so we can hammer in nails. We use bicycles, cars, phones, and aeroplanes to reach further and faster than we can with our bodies. We see these external tools as a part of ourselves. Cooking takes some of the internal process of digestion and takes it out into the world, expanding on the range of foods that can be metabolised.

We similarly metabolise ideas and thoughts outside our brains. We externalise memory with shopping lists and bus timetables and use laptops with their digital memory. We put up street signs as indicators of where we are and use traffic lights to know when to go and stop. We even use our bodies when we count with our fingers.

Just as any tool can be used for good or bad, so can the ways we extend cognition into the world. Passwords can be hacked, identities stolen, and written information can be stolen, destroyed, or used to blackmail.

Seeing cognition within a 4e framework tells us that cognition can only happen with an environment to experience, a body to sense, a brain to make sense, and a body to enact a response. In essence, cognition and life are unitary processes without boundaries.

Experience is a Construction

I look at a clock and hear it go tick-tock. What I hear is not the clock. The clock, whatever that actually is out in the world, sends out data announcing itself. Light bounces off the clock and comes to my eyes. Sound waves are sent out because of the mechanical movements of the clock that travel to my ear. What reaches my senses is not the clock itself but waves of light and sound at different frequencies. The sounds, sights, and other senses reach my sense organs, where they are coded into electrical signals that travel along nerve fibres to the brain. Again, these electrical signals are not the clock. The electrical signals are processed to create an experience I have of a clock going tick-tock. The experience is generated because of the clock. If the clock changes, the experience changes, but what I experience is totally different from the clock in the world. What I experience is created in my mind. What I experience can only ever be a representation of the outside world. A photograph can tell us much about a scene, but it will never be the scene. It is never more than coloured dots on paper. We can never know what the world is really like, and we can never fully know anybody else's experience. There is no way to know that what I call red is what you call red, even if we both agree that something is red, or even a particular shade of red.

I feel and hear my heart beating lub-dub, but if you think about it, it is still no more real than the clock out there going tick-tock. My heart is inside my body, so it feels more real. It is *my* heart, but the heart is still a "thing" out there, outside the brain, that sends coded electrical signals along nerve fibres to the brain. As with the clock, the brain processes electrical signals to generate an experience of a beating heart, but the experience is no more real than the experience of the clock. Experience happens in our mind even if we feel it in our body.

This means that there is no boundary between what is inside me and what is outside of me. Both are just representations formed from perturbations outside the brain. It is useful to be clear about the difference between the mind and the brain. The brain is the squishy organic material; the mind is what we can't touch but is nevertheless real. My heart and the clock are both outside the brain, but the brain is also a part of the body. We have always been brought up to assume our mind is in our head because our brain is in our head, but it need not be. Then our whole experience of the outside world and our body all arises as one, inseparably from our mind.

Figure 3.2 A recycle bin and a folder. What is seen is just a mass of changing coloured dots, but the impact of dragging the file to the recycle bin has implications in the real world. Author's photograph.

The world is not the way we think it is, but those convenient untruths make acting in the world possible. My body and the world I live in are convenient constructions of mind. It makes sense of Immanuel Kant's idea that mind creates time and space to experience consciousness.[8]

Another analogy that makes the same point is that of a computer. The monitor is like our mind. It is the interface between the outside world and the inside world. The keyboard and computer user are the outside world, and the inside world is the motherboard and the central processing unit (CPU). The monitor is only a large collection of changing coloured dots arranged so the dots produce an understandable image for the computer user, as in Figure 3.2. There might be a file on the desktop. We understand it as a file and treat it as a file with information we can access, but it is only a collection of dots created from signals coming from the motherboard.

Our mind similarly creates representations of the world we treat as if they were real. If I double-click on the dots in the shape of a file on the screen, I can access useful information even if the image is not real. Just as there is no clock in my brain there is no document in the computer, only encoded electrical signals. Similarly, the electrical information held in neural loops in the brain is invisible to us but holds information in ways we do not yet understand.

Another image on the screen is the recycle bin, which is merely another collection of dots. I can use the mouse to pick up the file and move it to the recycle bin. All that changes on the screen is dots changing colour, but they trigger changes in the electrical connections in the CPU. This has real-world consequences because the information is no longer accessible, other than by restoring it from the bin. If it is deleted from the bin, it is gone forever.

In the same way, electrical signals have been sent back and forth in my brain, leading to body movements with real-world implications. With an understanding of how we create our experience, we move on to an examination of the challenges of living systems co-operating for mutual benefit.

Managing Conflict

When a living system or organisation starts, it is less complex and less connected. The difference that makes a difference between the parts is low. I am in a small men's group, depicted below in Figure 3.3. There are no complex tasks. Everything is simple. Everyone gets a voice, and a consensus of the whole group emerges easily. Any differences can be talked through. We need no infrastructure, and nobody is in charge. It feels like paradise compared to larger, heavily bureaucratic organisations.

We sometimes look upon early civilisations such as the Greeks as living in a Golden Age before life became complex and violent. Our childhood is often seen as a carefree, magical time of life. A business starting is exciting and new. It is still flexible and relatively simple. Anything seems possible. Risks can be taken that cannot be taken later. This can lead to romanticising earlier times when life was easy. It is the honeymoon time before things become complex and going back becomes impossible.

Each new opportunity creates more opportunities. Growth at this point is typically exponential. Living systems tend to keep expanding until a constraining factor slows them down. As living and social systems grow and learn, they need more and more energy to sustain themselves.

If we consider a system with 10 members, there are 10×10 interconnections between the parts, making 100 connections.[9] If we add one more

Figure 3.3 My men's group at a weekend retreat. I am in the front with the talking stick.   Photograph by Ange Palmer.

member (one person is a 10% increase), there are 11 members, but the number of connections to be maintained is 11 × 11 = 121. One new member means 21 new connections, which is a 21% increase. And if you add four members to the 10 there are 14 members (a 40% increase in size but 14 × 14 = 196 connections), which is a 96% increase in interconnections to be maintained. As you see, even small increases in the size of a group can greatly increase the complexity of the interactions.

So, difference creates variety, which creates opportunity. But difference also creates conflict to be resolved. When requisite variety is still low, conflict tends to be low. Conflict builds quickly as the system becomes increasingly complex. That lag felt in the Golden Age before complexity grabs hold creates the illusion of paradise, but it cannot last. Conflict arises both within the living system and between the system and the environment.

Conflict can be resolved in positive ways that enhance those concerned. At best, a solution is found where both parties achieve more than they could have alone. In barn raising, a whole community comes together to build a barn for one farmer very quickly. No farmer could build a barn alone, but each farmer has a turn until everyone has a barn. When goals clash, conflict is harder to resolve. Compromise allows a mutual benefit such as selling a car. The buyer had to pay more than they wanted, and the seller received less, but a compromising deal was possible. An impasse means the gap between the desires of both parties is too great. Finally, there are zero-sum interactions where one wins at the expense of the other. The outcome is less likely to be positively resolved and may devolve into violence.

Since error is inherent in all life, there will inevitably be times when situations are not well resolved, such as when goals are misunderstood, incorrect motives are attributed, or there is malicious intent. While we cannot eradicate difference and conflict, we can develop more effective ways of resolving conflict.

A complex system creates order from chaos. We can see conflict as chaos to be resolved. Too much order leads to rigidity and too little order leads to deep chaos, where nothing can be sustained. There is a point of dynamic balance between order and chaos just before a system lapses into deep chaos, called the *edge of chaos* (Figure 3.4). A runner can run in an orderly fashion with little risk that anything will go wrong, but they will be slow. As they run faster, the risk increases, and their running becomes more chaotic. There is a balance point when the runner runs at an optimum speed where the risk of lapsing into deep chaos and falling or tripping is acceptable. At any moment they could come across an uneven piece of ground or a stone that causes them to trip; however, the gains of running faster are perceived as greater than the small risk of an injury while falling.

In practice, living permanently at the edge of chaos is too stressful, so living systems tend to operate as near as they feel comfortable enough to the

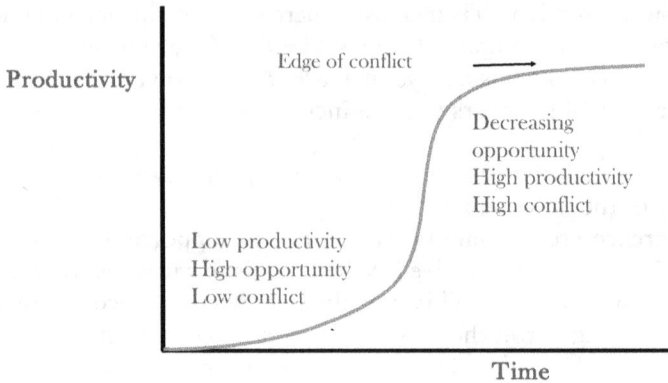

Figure 3.4 An S-curve showing high initial growth due to variety, which is slowed by increasing conflict levelling off at the edge of conflict.

edge of chaos. They venture to the edge for a while when it feels safe enough and then pull back again. They still, however, sometimes misjudge the edge and tip over into deep chaos.

Sometimes a system at the edge of chaos may spontaneously self-organise within itself to function in a new, more complex, and previously unpredictable way. Emergent behaviour can arise from the edge of chaos as parts form a new whole.

There is a similar point I call the *edge of conflict*, which exhibits the same dance between variety and conflict that we see between order and chaos. A system moves to increase variety, but as it does so it approaches the edge of conflict. There is a point at which the system is willing to accept the risk of conflict even if it could become violent. Just like the edge of chaos, staying at the edge permanently is too stressful for living systems and they hover as near as is comfortable. In the same way that we sometimes need to take a reasonable risk, we must also live with reasonable conflict.

Think of times when you went near the edge of conflict and the situation, which could have become a catastrophe, turned into an opportunity because of your calm response to the situation. Then think of a situation where the interaction went past the edge of conflict into deep chaos or deep conflict.

In New Zealand, the open road speed limit is 100 km/hr. It generally means around 300 people die each year through road accidents. This is considered an acceptable reasonable risk to enable convenient travel. If the speed limit were reduced to 50km/h, road deaths would plummet. Developed countries find it acceptable for people in the developing world to live in poverty, with high levels of pollution and health risks so the West can continue in an ultimately unsustainable way of life.

Systems often find themselves in a Darwinian fight for fitness in their environment. If others prove fitter, they will struggle to survive. A creature that is prepared to live at or near the edge of conflict will gain fitness over other creatures that are more cautious. In effect, living systems have no choice but to embrace conflict and the risk of violence to avoid being pushed out of their niche.

As a living system becomes more complex, typically at least one resource becomes scarce and thus contestable. Remembering the group of people coming to an unexplored island in Chapter 1, we noted that initially there was rapid growth until land became a contested resource. Greed is not a problem until there are scarce resources. As soon as there is scarcity, there must be a decision about how the resources are to be divided up. Using violence is one way of claiming a scarce resource.

Even societies we might see as peaceful and harmonious have a hidden face of violence. Tibetan Buddhists are portrayed as peaceful people living virtuous lives, but the monastic tradition was based on a feudal structure with peasants producing the surplus that enabled the monasteries to exist. The Dalai Lamas in earlier times were both political and religious leaders, ruling a nation with warlike Chinese neighbours. Some of the actions of earlier Dalai Lamas appear as an anathema to the Dalai Lama as he lives today.

Difference Creates Inequality

As a group grows larger, variety increases, and conflict and complexity grow. This also creates greater inequality between the parts. The range of difference from the bottom to the top widens. Imagine that 100 people are each given $10,000 to create more value. Even though they all start with the same amount, some will do better than others. Sometimes it will be through skill and good planning; at other times it will be sheer good luck. Over time, the outcomes will be different. After a time, some will have $12,000 and others $8,000. Those with $12,000 will find it easier than those with $8,000 to further develop and will tend to prosper even more while those with $8,000 will tend to do worse. Over time, the inequality will grow in ways that create fractal patterns with a few people with extreme wealth and most people with much less. The spread of inequality is described by *Pareto's Law*,[10] often known as the 80-20 rule. This states that roughly 20% of the people will end up owning 80% of the resources. Sometimes this is also called the Matthew Effect after the biblical quote of Jesus, "For to everyone who has shall more be given, and he shall have an abundance; but from the one who does not have, even what he does have shall be taken away" (Matthew 25:29, New King James version).

The whole structure of capitalism as a way of distributing resources in a society moves towards increased inequality. The gap between the haves and the have-nots grows wider and wider. There comes a point where the system feeds on itself so much its future viability is in question.

Co-ordinators and Leaders

A men's group of eight people works well without an infrastructure, but a group of 200 cannot work in the same way. There is simply not enough time for everyone to talk. As a group becomes more complex, it must reorganise itself to cope with the increased entropy and chaos it encounters. At all levels of life, smaller subgroups (*coordinators*) are formed by choice or force to make decisions on behalf of the whole. The small group has less entropy, so it can generally manage the conflict. Sometimes that coordinating subgroup group is not able to manage the level of disorder and chaos, so a higher layer (*leader*) is formed above it. The system can keep adding layers until the energy is sufficiently dispersed, but each layer increases the inequality, and higher layers are often increasingly disconnected from lower layers. Robert Michels[11] states the Iron Law of Oligarchy as, "Whoever says organisation, says oligarchy". He contends that organised human activity inevitably leads to a small group taking power.

The top layer holds the authority to define the group purpose, which is aligned with the official rule set. The authority structure is legitimised. The purpose of the group acts as an attractor, pulling together the disparate parts towards achieving a common goal. Reward and punishment structures operate to keep the system within the limits that provide enough coherence for the system to maintain itself.

Rules can become so ingrained over time as to become unnoticeable. Norbert Elias[12] wrote about a book on etiquette and manners written in the 1500s, which found it necessary to advise people that it was bad manners to defecate on your dining chair and wipe your bottom on the curtain. That rule has become so internalised that it now appears comical to mention it.

The tendency for people to be selfish and only think of themselves must be overcome to maintain group cohesion. Societal influence rewards generosity, sacrificing for others, upholding agreements and traditions, and remaining calm in difficult situations. In Māori society, *mana* accrues to people who contribute to the life of the tribe. This social capital can be stored for a time when assistance is needed from others. The concept of *koha*, or gifting to others, is critical to maintain tribal coherence within and between tribes.

Leadership is the skill of containing the disorder that others do not contain. A leader steps forth to coordinate activities in order to create order. There are many styles of leadership from a command-and-control style out front that makes inequality more evident, through to supportive leadership styles that encourage others to take leadership. Mana increases when people think of the group's needs before their own.

Primary and Shadow Systems

Just as shining a light on an object automatically creates a shadow, when we form a vision or purpose that leads to a rule set, we open the space for an opposing story to emerge. As soon as we establish a primary story, a shadow story constellates in the background. When the government proposes a policy, it invites opposition from other parties. Carl Jung used the term *shadow* to represent those aspects of ourselves that we are unwilling or unable to integrate into our being. A shadow is dark and ever-present.

There is a resonance with Newton's Law of Motion, which states that every action creates an equal and opposite reaction. Sir Geoffrey Vickers[13] used the metaphor of a rocking boat to demonstrate this. A small boat is tied at the wharf. It is still and steady. As soon as someone steps in, the boat moves in response and unless the person stepping in moves to compensate for the reaction they started, they risk falling in the water. Every step to rebalance sets off more rocking. If another person steps into the boat, the rocking becomes even less predictable and harder to control.

Life needs something to push against to move. It is by taking on challenges and grappling with conflict that we grow and achieve. Our muscles grow strong when we use them to do things.

Chinese philosophy describes yin and yang as two forces in nature. These might seem to be opposing forces, but the reality is more subtle. There is always some yang in the yin and yin in the yang. When we take anything to the extreme, it becomes its own opposite.

It is often useful to consider the complementary view in any situation. So often it is equally valid and adds a necessary counterbalance. I might say, "I am my own person, I can do what I want." That is true, but it is just as true to say, "I need to fit in with the people around me and consider their needs."

The coordinating and leader subsystems are complete systems in their own right within the living and social system. That means they have their own purpose and rule set, primary and shadow story, and their own unresolved disorder that is sent back into the system or expelled outside. Other subsystems emerge within the living system. A community might include subgroups

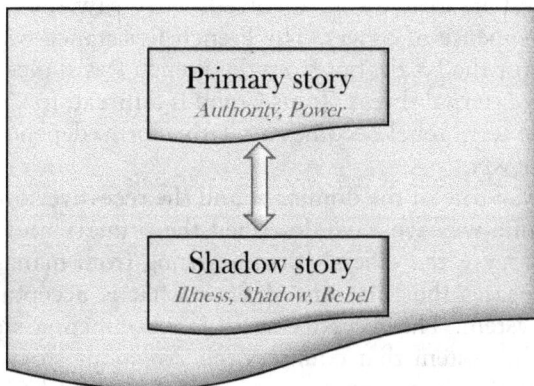

Figure 3.5 As soon as a primary story is established, a shadow story starts to be formulated in response to the primary story.

with particular cultures, religions, special interests, political orientations, or whatever. They will all need to manage the difference between their rule set and the rule set of the larger living system of which they are a part. Living systems have fractal natures, not only as systems of systems but also subsystems of subsystems within those systems. Rather than one linear chain of subsystems, we find a dense network of systems and subsystems. We could say Nelson Province is a subsystem of New Zealand and Nelson City is a subsystem of Nelson Province. Still, we can equally say that within New Zealand culture is Māori culture, within that is Kāi Tahu culture, and within that is Kāti Kuri culture. Within the whole population of the LGBTQIA+ community is the transgender community.

Because there is an autonomy–connectivity tension in all living systems, there will be times when parts act in their own interests rather than the whole, or they have allegiances to other groups with competing purposes. That will lead to rebellious actions that defy the rules established by the leading group. They will form the *other* within the system. Rebels can collaborate to form a shadow subsystem. They might even make alliances with groups outside the system to help their cause or form their own coordinating layer. The rebel group itself can have dissenters forming a shadow group within the shadow group. They may be more like the primary group or be even more extreme than the shadow group.

The rebel can be a freeloader, accepting the gains created by the group cohesion without contributing the expected effort or sacrifice. The rebel is often marginalised and rejected. We usually see a rebel as a negative element to be quashed and rendered powerless but in the Star Wars movies, for example, rebels are depicted as the resisting force against an evil external system. They try to stop the primary story to regain power and institute their worldview and rule set.

The Nazi regime demonstrated that a primary system and its rules are not always in the best interests of all involved. They saw their good as being achieved at the expense of others. The French Resistance was a part of the rebellious other for the Nazis, but from the French Resistance viewpoint, the Nazis formed an external threat. To us Covid is a threat; to Covid, we are an opportunity. The term rebel becomes a relative term, depending on the perspective of the viewer.

Ralph Stacey[14] wrote of the dominant and the recessive story in an organisation in the same way we have described the primary and shadow story. The dominant story is the official version arising from management leadership which delineates the rules and defines what is acceptable within the bounds of the system. The recessive story is a competing story that arises from lower in the system that counters the dominant story. The recessive story can disrupt the dominant story in good ways and bad. Innovation is more likely to arise from the recessive story. Often the dominant story is the theory of how things should be done, and the recessive story is what actually happens. Ideally, dominant and recessive groups can dialogue to generate healthy solutions.

Commonly, the clash in narratives between the dominant and recessive groups leads to taking positions, professing "I am right, and you are wrong", "You are the cause of the problem" and "Since you oppose the right I am doing, your work is evil". Once these entrenched positions are taken up, it becomes increasingly difficult to resolve underlying differences.

During the Covid crisis, mandates to wear masks or require vaccination led to organised opposition to the primary rule set. Think of times when you have noticed a shadow story emerge as a primary story unfolds.

Members who have assumed the role of coordinator or leader typically need or claim a reward for taking on the extra responsibility of their position, such as status, money, or sexual favours. The coordinator group takes on a mantle of legitimacy to use the power it has been ceded. They have greater access to resources, power, and information than those outside the subsystem. It is tempting for them to put their personal needs and desires of their subsystem above the needs of the whole system. They become their own shadow and generate resentment. Once an organisational structure is formed, maintaining that structure can become more important than the vision that brought it about.

The leadership group must meet the ongoing needs of the members more effectively than the members could have provided for themselves. The members must have an adequate share of energy, matter, and information to maintain their well-being. The leadership group must organise the distribution of energy, matter, and information to members and ensure the ongoing protection of the group members from internal or external influences that might cause harm. The coordinating and leadership groups need effective monitoring systems to provide information about the system's effectiveness to make the necessary decisions so the system can cope with its challenges.

Members are concerned with day-to-day issues, the coordinators perhaps weeks and months, while leaders look years in advance. Decisions should be made at the appropriate level. Deciding high enough up the hierarchy usually means that those making the decision have sufficient skills, resources, and overview to respond adequately. Making decisions too high up leaves leaders making trivial decisions distracting them from their true purpose.

The *Dynamics of Life* Model

We are finally at the point where we can combine all these ideas and concepts into the *Dynamics of Life* model. The model has three parts: the Dynamics of Life diagram; the Tree of Life; and the Adaptive Cycle. Together they provide a comprehensive mapping applicable at all levels of functioning for living systems. The rest of this book reveals how this overarching concept fits at each level of life.

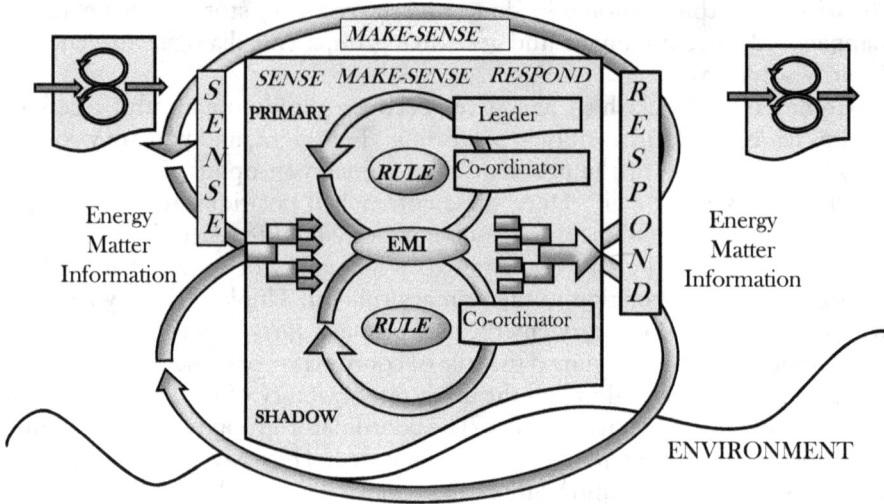

Figure 3.6 The Dynamics of Life diagram shows flows of energy, matter, and information. This model fits all levels of living systems from a single cell to the entire planet.

The Dynamics of Life diagram shown in Figure 3.6 reveals how energy, matter, and information flow through a living system using fractal formations for efficiency. The flow is contained and processed through the rule set imposed on the system. Sometimes levels of hierarchy (coordinator and leader and more) are needed to manage all the energy, matter, and information as depicted in the top primary loop inside the living system.

There can be difference that cannot be processed even at the top level which again increases disorder to be managed. If there is too much unprocessed conflict and difference, the living system will become unhealthy and may die.

The living system does work through the body to change the environment. This is the top loop outside the creature. Whatever is done impacts the world and prompts a response, that again generates difference to be managed.

As soon as a rule set is imposed, there will be a reaction against the rule set. There will be rebels opposing which form the shadow system (that loops downwards). There is a shadow loop inside the system and a shadow loop in the environment. The shadow loops generate more difference to be contained.

No living system can use all the energy, matter, and information it takes in. Some is always lost or unusable. Whatever energy, matter, or information that is not processed is passed on by being projected elsewhere. Some waste is expelled into the environment but some remains in the living system to become toxic, usually in the shadow system.

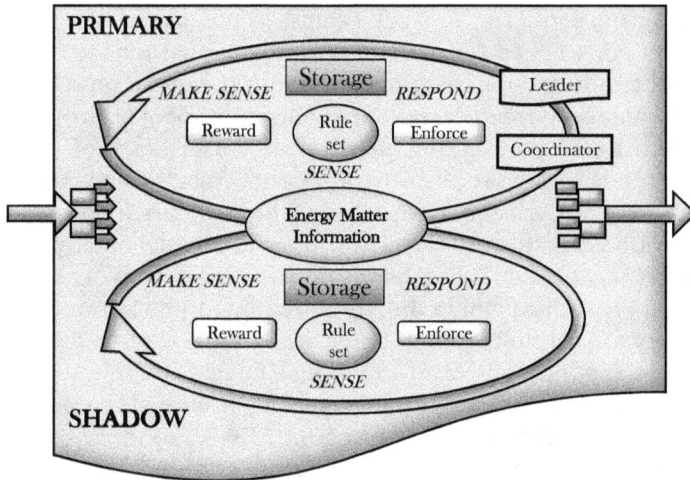

Figure 3.7 Inside the system energy, matter, and information is stored for later use. Rewards and punishment maintain the rule set.

You will notice a double figure-eight shape. Inside is a primary circle and a shadow circle forming a figure-eight describing internal processes and an external primary and shadow loop for processes interacting in the environment. Figure 3.7 shows more detail about what happens within the system.

Inside the living or social system, there is storage. Matter is stored that might be fat cells or silos of grain held by a community. Energy is stored in those fat cells or in a battery or petrol for a vehicle. Information is stored in memory on signs, or in a computer. It can be later retrieved, but there is always a loss over time of energy, matter, and information due to entropy. The rule set is ensured by rewarding compliance and punishing defiance. With the diagram complete, the next step is to understand how it functions at the different levels of life.

The Tree of Life

The Tree of Life is the second part of the model, which takes the diagram formulated above and places it in context. We start this second part with an overview of the evolution of life, which has led to human beings and our social organisations.

Evolution

When resources are scarce, living systems compete to gain the necessary resources or risk losing fitness compared to their competitors and may die. Living systems adapt and learn new skills rapidly but so does the competition, creating a ratcheting effect that increases fitness in that environment.

At times, evolution seems to work against us because what was optimal at one time was not so later. Our bodies are still adapted for life on the savannah in small family groups foraging and hunting, but we now live in apartments with mobile phones, cars, and millions of people around us. This mismatch has led to poor eating, depressive illnesses, lack of exercise, and many other modern-day problems that disconnect us from ourselves.

Evolution cannot erase previous layers, because the living system must always stay alive. It adds new layers on top of the old, sometimes resulting in clumsy arrangements. When hands and fingers first evolved, they were used to grasp branches, which only required one signal from the brain for all the fingers to curl up together. Later, when we were living on the plains making tools, having control of individual fingers became useful. Rather than taking out the hand curl signal to replace it with a new set of instructions, we can only modify the old pattern. If I wish to move one finger the signal to curl my whole hand is sent as before and then, a second signal is sent instructing the other fingers to ignore the last signal, so only the selected finger ends up doing the grasping action. That is why it is almost impossible to move only one finger or several fingers without moving the others at least a little. Try touching your little finger and thumb without moving your ring finger!

Evolution is commonly depicted as a straight line with one event or one species after the other or depicted as a tree from the earliest life forms through until today, but that is a simplified picture. Rather than a tree with one trunk, the reality is more like a network with many side branches that sometimes come back and sometimes do not. Evolution does not just occur vertically from generation to generation. There are horizontal processes like hybridising and horizontal gene transfer that affect evolution.

Evolution has often arisen through slow changes over time but sometimes there are sudden jumps. This might have occurred as *exaptation*,[15] where something that evolved for one task suddenly fits for another. Bird feathers originally evolved to keep them warm, but they fortuitously evolved in such a way as to enable flight. Old car tyres work well tied to the side of a wharf to stop boats banging against the wharf.

Sometimes, when under pressure a creature may adapt by finding an entirely new way of responding to what happens. It is a new, emergent way of adapting that could not have been previously predicted. It is a sudden leap to a new level of functioning.

In this way, life has jumped through history up from the biological level of life to the psychological level of mind, to the cultural level of the social. Each new level means greater complexity and a greater energy flow to maintain it. As a reptile, a crocodile does not need much energy to sustain itself, but its capabilities are limited. A chimpanzee needs far more energy and is far more complex. It has a much wider repertoire of behaviours to cope with life's challenges.

A consequence of these adaptive leaps is the formation of hierarchies. Higher levels arise that are more complex and enlarge the system's capacity but require greater energy flows. Higher does not always mean better. There are always trade-offs. We have lost useful capacities that our early ancestors had such as their sense of connectedness with nature.

Four Levels of Hierarchy

Gregg Henriques describes a four-phase hierarchy through which humanity evolved. The foundational layer is that of matter. First, *matter* appeared on earth, controlled by the laws of physics and chemistry. Out of that arose *life* as simple living creatures controlled by complex system dynamics. *Mind* evolved in minded animals. From mind, *culture* emerged as humans formed shared belief systems and stories. We could be evolving towards a spiritual level of functioning through the fifth joint point. The levels are all linked and co-exist in a symbiotic relationship as in Figure 3.8.

Matter is studied using physics and chemistry. Life is analysed using biology. Mind is studied using psychology and culture comes under sociology and anthropology. The world of matter is controlled by the laws of motion. If you can measure something accurately enough, you can predict its motion. At the level of life, living systems must still obey the laws of physics. They remain subject to gravity. Complex adaptive systems, and thus all living systems, have new constraints enabling much more complex behaviours. Derek Cabrera developed his DSRP model mentioned in Chapter 1, which describes the cognitive world of living systems as having four core principles: distinctions, systems, relationships, and perspectives. The parts of a system emerge

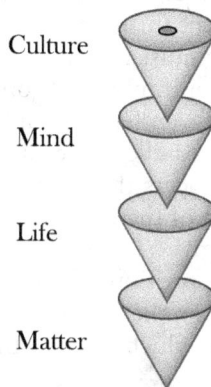

Figure 3.8 Gregg Henriques' Tree of Knowledge shows the emergent levels of matter, life, mind, and culture. Note where the fifth joint point depicts where the realm of spirit might emerge.   Reprinted with permission of Gregg Henriques.

from the distinctions that arise when a boundary is set. The parts interact to form a system. Parts form relationships with each other, and each part has its unique perspective.

Each level from matter to culture arises out of the previous level and cannot function without it as a foundation. Many authors have developed maps of human evolution and noted how they roughly resonate with the developmental levels of a single human being. As we individually grow and mature, our focus moves through the same stages from biology to psychology, to sociology, and then spirituality.

Each of the levels operates through flows of energy, matter, and information, and must manage disorder as it appears at each level. The disorder impacts differently at each level, but the same underlying patterns are exhibited.

At the physical level, food is metabolised to provide energy to operate the body. At the emotional level, the energy in the experience is processed as emotion, which motivates a person to act. At the thinking level, we make sense of information, comparing it to existing belief systems to act more effectively. Finally, we organise our actions socially with other people to enhance our capabilities. Each level expels disorder in its own way.

The Tree of Life diagram depicted in Figures 3.9 and 3.10 has branches representing the evolutionary layers of human development. All the branches are linked to the whole tree. No branch can exist alone. A branch without a tree is only good for firewood. The tree roots embody the underlying systems principles that constrain and shape what is possible for the whole tree. The Dynamics of Life structure describes life at each level.

Ken Wilber[16] writes of the principle of *transcend and include*. This means that as we move up a layer in evolutionary development, we include the lower levels. Higher levels cannot function without the foundation of previous levels. As we start to express emotions, we do not get rid of the body. Our body and the messages sent through the body have a big impact on the emotion that is expressed. We must maintain a healthy and vibrant body to feel our emotions. Similarly, our thinking sits on the foundations of body and emotions. We know whether we prefer to eat a burger or a pizza by reflecting on the emotion that each would elicit. We cannot decide without emotion. Thinking is not an isolated process that happens within the neurons of our brain. Without the foundation of the body within an environment and emotions, there can be no thinking.

As we move up a layer, the previous shadow does not go away, so as we transcend and include, we carry the shadow. As we form the new level, its shadow system starts to form, which links to the shadow system of the previous level.

Each level has its own primary and shadow cycles, and an inside and an outside. Any unresolved chaos or difference at one level can be passed up the hierarchy. If a worker can't fix a machine, they go to the supervisor. If the supervisor cannot help, they go to the engineer. They continue up the hierarchy until

Table 3.1 Shows how matter, energy, and information is processed at each level

	Process	Energy source	Production	Unresolved entropy	Impact of leakage	Rule set	Rewards	Enforcement
Spirit	Worship	God - universal intelligence	Inner peace	Disconnection cults	Clash of beliefs	Spiritual paradigm	Samadhi	Karma
Social	Organising	Communication	Coordinated activity	Conflict between people	Confusion and Miscommunication	Laws and constitutions Social etiquette	Social recognition Prizes Awards	Police Army
Thinking information	Making sense	Information	Concepts and ideas	Argument or doubt	Poor decision making	Belief and value system	Clarity of thought	Persuasion forced beliefs
Energy emotion	Expressing Emotions	Energy Experience	Action	Acting out	Suppressed emotion Trauma	Habit patterns	Positive emotion	Negative emotion
Biological	Metabolism	Food water	Energy	Bodily waste	Illness	Genetic algorithm Instinct	Pleasure	Pain
Physical								

INTERNAL

EXTERNAL

Spirit
Co-actualisation

Self or in group
Primary: Set a Rule or Law
Shadow: Opposition to rule

Social
Self esteem
culture

Community Organisation nation
Primary: Group acts
Shadow: External response

Self-talk Values and beliefs
Primary: Set intention
Shadow: Doubt

Thinking Clarity
beliefs and values

Dialogue
Primary: Express opinion
Shadow: Response to opinion

Feeling: Positive-negative emotion
Primary: Emotion arises
Shadow: Suppressed emotion

Emotion
Judgment

Expression of emotion
Primary: Express emotion outwardly
Shadow: Response to emotion

Sensation - Pain pleasure
Primary : intention to act
Shadow: Caution

Body
Safety

Movement
Primary: Move body
Shadow: Impact on world

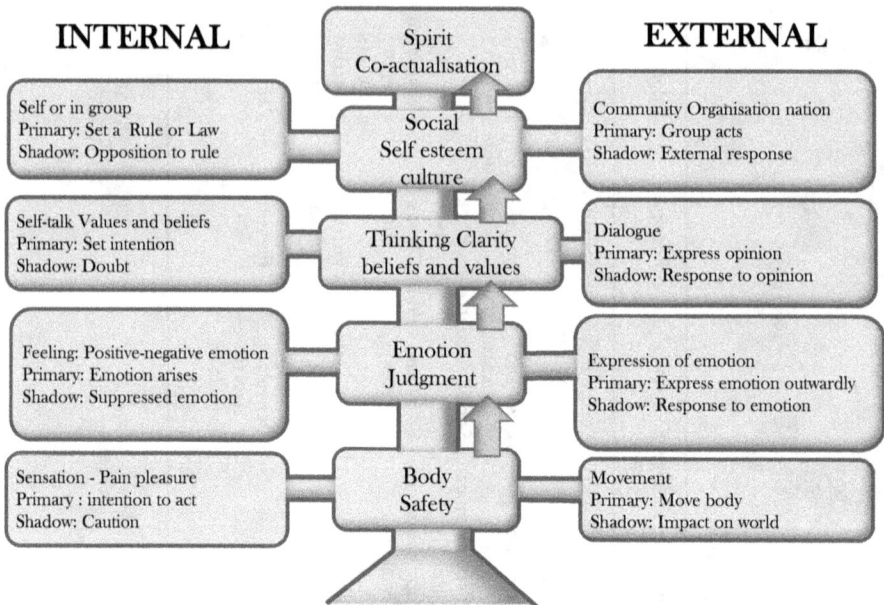

Figure 3.9 The Eros Tree of Life of creation and growth depicting internal and external worlds and primary and shadow aspects.

all free energy is contained. Ken Wilber calls this the *eros* function because it is growing and creative.

The symbol of a tree is apt because it demonstrates the separate levels, while simultaneously showing connections and interactions between them. It also shows that all levels are a part of the one tree. You may notice the central trunk is similar to Maslow's *Hierarchy of Needs* from survival to self-actualisation.[17] The top level here is spiritual, but it is the growing tip of the tree, not the top of the triangle, so it is open to grow and evolve. You will also notice it is labelled *co-actualisation* rather than self-actualisation because a person who is actualised lives their connectedness with others.

There are times when all levels of hierarchy have been used to contain the disorder, but entropy remains. All our body budget has been used and the living system moves into overwhelm. We make budget cuts to economise on our energy use. We move from eros to *thanatos*, the path of destruction and death, going down the tree instead of up as in Figure 3.9. Switching off a level saves bioenergy, but we lose the capabilities of that higher level. When we cannot organise a solution at the social level, we fall back to the thinking level, forcing our ideas onto others, and leading to arguments. If that does not work, we vent and rage at the emotional level. The final strategy, when all else has failed, is to physically fight. This happens for each of us individually and as societies and communities.

INTERNAL -
Maintenance

Spirit
Co-actualisation

EXTERNAL -
Work

Anarchy
Infighting factions

Social
Loss of vision
Power

Despotism
Blaming other
Stonewalling
Scapegoat

Inner critic muddled
thinking cognitive
distortions

Thinking
Confusion
Delusions
Personality disorder

Argument

Suppression

Emotion
Anxiety Psychotic
Neurotic

Acting out

Shock, freeze

Body
Stress tension
illness

Fight Flight

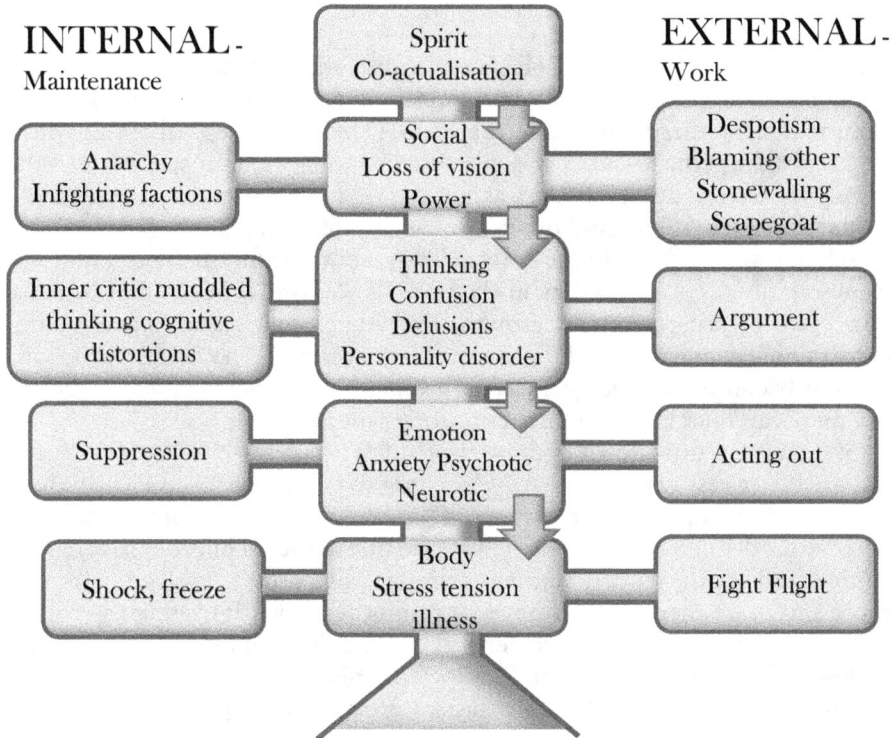

Figure 3.10 Thanatos, the tree of destruction and death. As we fail to maintain our existence, we drop back through levels until fighting and violence is the only strategy left.

There was a Māori land protest at Bastion Point (Takaparawha) in Auckland in 1977. Prime urban land was stolen from the rightful Māori owners and sold for property development. Attempts to use social means to negotiate an agreement failed. Māori occupied the land for 506 days before police arrested them. A kilometre or so down the road, armed soldiers were ready to implement the final act of violence to assert the dominant authority. Eventually, the land was returned to the people of Ngāti Whātua Ōrākei.

The final part of the model is to investigate how living systems change over time. Life has a cycle to it. Life breathes in and out in cycles. We have already seen that a living system starts in an immature form that is not well connected. As the system connects, exponential growth takes off. Eventually, the system becomes constrained and rigid, so the parts disconnect again and break down to start a new cycle. The Adaptive Cycle formulated by Buzz Holling and Lance Gunderson[18] describes this cycle of life and fits in with the *Dynamics of Life* model.

The Adaptive Cycle

The Adaptive Cycle is a four-phase cycle observed in complex adaptive systems. The four phases are exploitation (sometimes called growth), conservation, release, and reorganisation (Figure 3.11). The concept of the adaptive cycle grew from the research and measurement of ecological systems, but the principles were found to be just as applicable to economic systems, human systems, social systems, and other complex adaptive systems.

A living system starts in the bottom left quadrant from small beginnings to grow rapidly (exploitation) as in the post-World War II boom that began a new cycle of prosperity and growth. Everything grows and expands until constraining factors slow the growth (conservation). The system grows so much it becomes cumbersome and inflexible. A small boat can turn quickly, but an ocean liner takes kilometres to turn around.

Systems also slow down because we tend to "pick the low-hanging fruit". We use the easiest resources first. Why climb to the top of the tree when there are plenty of apples at the bottom? This means picking apples later will become harder and require more effort. We first gathered oil from easy, cheap sources and left the more dangerous and expensive sources until later. It takes more and more energy to get the same results as before. It eventually reaches the point where it takes as much energy to gain the resources they provide.

Joseph Tainter calls this the Law of Diminishing Returns[19] as shown in Figure 3.12, which depicts how a system grows in effectiveness until a constraining factor kicks in. The system cannot continue as it did before and

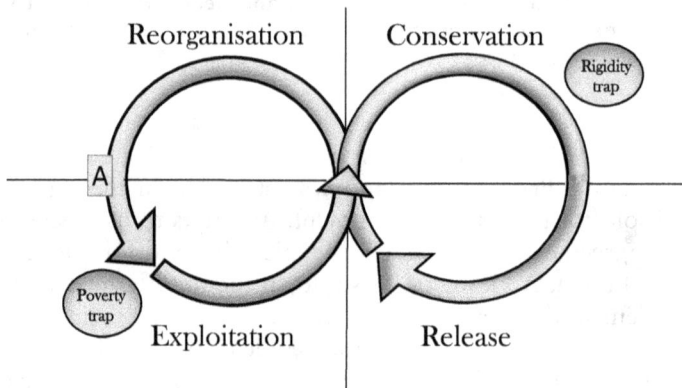

Figure 3.11 The Adaptive Cycle. The lower left quadrant is the exploitation/growth phase that grows quickly, but slows in the conservation phase and comes apart in the release phase. The system then reorganises itself to prepare for a new cycle. The diagram is three-dimensional, so the release/reorganisation phase does not cross over the exploitation/conservation phase but goes behind. Also note the position of point A, to which we will later return. Adapted from Panarchy edited by Lance H Gunderson and CS Holling. Copyright ©Island Press. Reproduced by permission of Island Press, Washington DC.

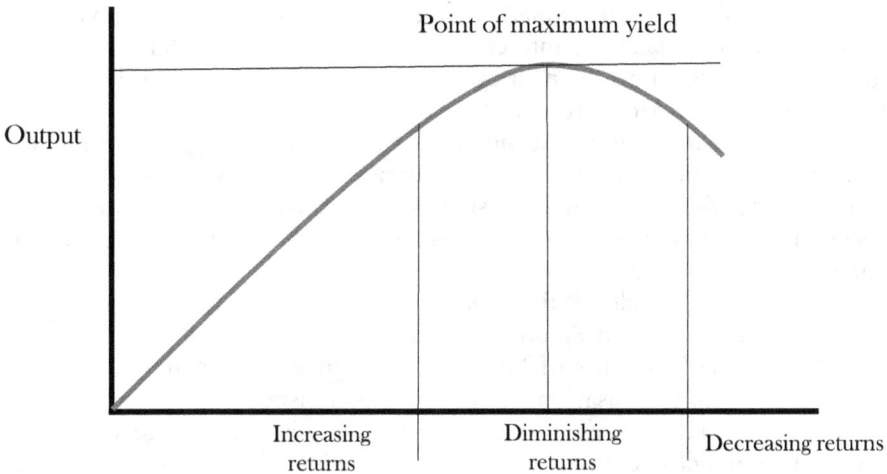

Point of maximum yield

Output

Increasing returns | Diminishing returns | Decreasing returns

Figure 3.12 At first, growth is very rapid. But the growth rate slows, and the curve flattens as the cost of gaining benefits increases. It then heads down until the cost of producing is unsustainable. Wikipedia Happy Avocado, https://commons.wikimedia.org/wiki/File:Diminishing_Returns_Graph.svg

must release and break some of the bonds that held it together (release) in the bottom right quadrant of Figure 3.11.

Very commonly when a system is struggling to maintain itself, it will find scapegoats on whom to blame the looming demise and who typically carry the cost the system is unwilling to pay. Hitler blamed the Jews, Stalin blamed dissidents, and capitalism makes the developing countries pay the cost of cheap consumer goods.

At the point it becomes unsustainable, things fall apart. The descent into the release phase is often rapid. The body of a person with cancer cells will adapt to keep functioning and apply patch after patch. Eventually, we run out of patches and the body quickly deteriorates. A *tipping point*[20] has been reached. Climate change is more likely to be rapid once it is triggered and the Earth's self-correcting mechanisms are all used up. The release phase can be positive, as in the struggle of an alcoholic to maintain sobriety rather than descending into another round of drinking. More typically, the release phase is experienced as loss and destruction.

The conservation phase may be prolonged, taking the system into the *rigidity trap*. The dynamics are distorted to prevent or delay the descent into the release phase. A business monopoly or use of military force may maintain a system that would otherwise have descended into release. When the system finally does descend, it is even more rapid and destructive.

After the release, we must pick up the remaining pieces to reorganise and start the cycle over again. A new cycle is initiated. The reorganisation phase is vital. There must be lessons learned or the same problems will arise on the next cycle. Political revolutionaries are often so focused on their revolution that little thought has gone into constructing a new world after, so the "hot potato" just passes into the next cycle. Napoleon, Stalin, and Hitler all rose to power with a lack of foresight during the previous reorganisation phase.

The *poverty trap* sits to the side of the reorganisation phase. In this the system survives but does not have the momentum to move into a new cycle as in a ghetto. Sometimes an ecosystem will drop from a vibrant interplay of species to a sustainable, but simpler balance with fewer species. It lacks the energy to restore the previous diversity.

The figure-eight cycles of the *Dynamics of Life* model and the figure eight of the Adaptive Cycle in Figure 3.11 are linked. The figure eight in Figure 3.13 linking the Dynamics of Life to the Adaptive Cycle starts at the mid-point A. First, an organisational structure is established to bring order to the chaos as the circle curves upward. As it grows, it struggles to cope with increasing conflict and moves around the circle into the conservation phase. The shadow system becomes apparent as the energy flows to the lower circle. As with the Adaptive Cycle, the flow is depicted three-dimensionally, so the line goes under point A and not through it, around the shadow cycle through the release and reorganisation phases, and back to point A again.

We can also see life as the process of connecting and disconnecting. At first, the parts grow, connect, and explore finding that they gain by collaborating. But connecting brings other tensions to the fore that leads to

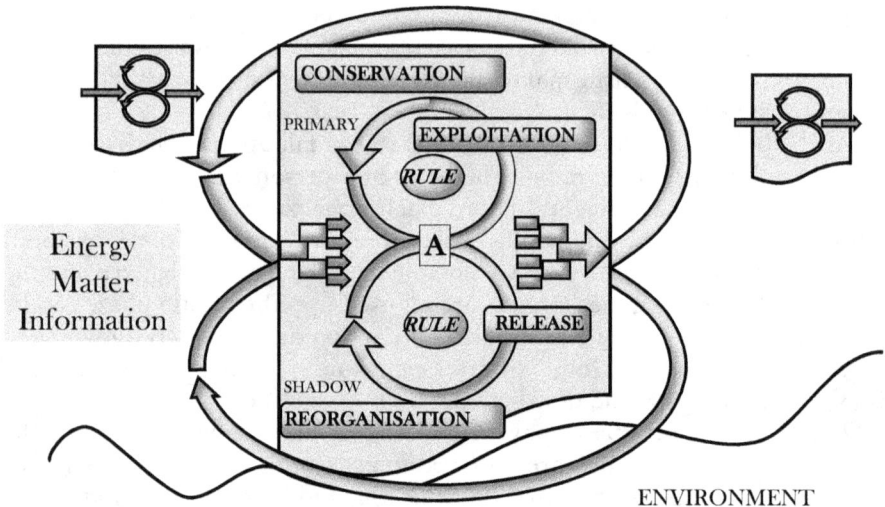

Figure 3.13 The adaptive cycle seen as a figure-eight movement within the *Dynamics of Life* model. Note that point A has been moved a quarter-turn from Figure 3.10 to align these two charts and that the figure eight is again three-dimensional.

disconnection. This culminates in a new cycle, where the parts come together in different arrangements that are hopefully more effective than before. The magic of life is in knowing when and how to connect and disconnect.

The *Dynamics of Life* model applies to life from the single cell and even into the atomic and subatomic realms through to human beings, families, communities, and nations. It also describes flows of history, economic systems, and ecological systems. How does the *Dynamics of Life* model relate to your life? Think of examples in your life that can be described and understood using the model.

With the *Dynamics of Life* model established, we can now delve into how it can be used to understand real-life situations. It is time to move from more abstract principles to how those principles manifest in human beings with biological, psychological, and social aspects.

Key Points

1 Cognition arises from the body.
2 All living systems anticipate the future.
3 Cognition is embodied, embedded, enactive, and extended.
4 Experience is a construction.
5 Life evolved through three main leaps from the biological to the psychological to the social.
6 Living systems start small without infrastructure but quickly become complex.
7 Difference creates variety, which creates opportunity, but difference also creates conflict.
8 Living systems grow towards the edge of conflict.
9 Conflict can be resolved positively as collaboration or negatively as violence.
10 Different creates inequality that over time fits the Pareto Law.
11 As living systems become more complex, they form a co-ordinator and management level to cope with the disorder.
12 As soon as a rule is established, the space is opened for a rebellion against the rules.
13 A healthy system is not necessarily a good system. The Nazi regime functioned efficiently but destroyed other systems.
14 The Dynamics of Life has three parts: The Dynamics of Life diagram, the Tree of Life and the Adaptive Cycle.
15 The Dynamics of Life diagram shows how energy, matter, and information flow through a living system.
16 The Tree of Life shows the levels of evolution for human beings with both a creative and growing form and a destructive form.
17 The Adaptive Cycle is a four-stage cycle of life where parts connect (exploitation) until the conflict rises (conservation) until the system divides (release) and the parts reorganise (reorganisation) for a new cycle.

Notes

1 See *The Feeling of What Happens: Body and Emotion in the Making of Consciousness* by Antonio Damasio.
2 Maturana and Varela call this *Structural Coupling*.
3 See *The Presentation of the Everyday Self* by Erving Goffman.
4 See Louie's description of Rosen's *Anticipation Systems Theory*.
5 See also *The Experience Machine* by Andy Clark and *Predictive Coding Under the Free Energy Principle* by Karl Friston.
6 See *Mind in Life* by Ewan Thompson and *The Oxford Handbook of 4e Cognition* by Leon de Bruin, Shaun Gallagher, and Albert Newen.
7 See *The Tree of Knowledge* by Humberto Maturana and Francisco Varela.
8 See *Critique of Pure Reason* by Immanuel Kant.
9 This is simplified to make the point. In fact, in a group of ten, each person only has nine connections with others in the group, since the connection to themselves is not counted. The mathematics is, therefore, more complicated but bears out the same general point.
10 This is a special case of Power Law Dynamics.
11 See *Political Parties: A Sociological Study of the Oligarchical Tendencies of Modern Democracy* by Robert Michels.
12 See *The Civilizing process: Sociogenetic and Psychogenetic Investigations* in Elias et al.
13 See *Freedom in a Rocking Boat: Changing Values in an Unstable Society* by Sir Geoffrey Vickers.
14 See *Complexity and Creativity in Organisations* by Ralph Stacey.
15 See *The Panda's Thumb* by Stephen Jay Gould.
16 See *Integral Psychology: Consciousness, Spirit, Psychology, Therapy* by Ken Wilber.
17 See *A Theory of Human Motivation* by Abraham Maslow.
18 See *Panarchy* by Buzz Holling and Lance Gunderson.
19 See *The Collapse of Complex Societies* by Joseph Tainter.
20 See *The Tipping Point: How Little Things Can Make a Big Difference* by Malcolm Gladwell.

Bibliography

Cabrera, D., & Cabrera, L. (2015). *Systems Thinking Made Simple; New Hope for Solving Wicked Problems*. Cabrera Research Lab.

Clark, A. (2024). *The Experience Machine: How our Minds Predict and Shape Reality*. (Herauitgave Edition). Penguin Books.

Damasio, A. (1994). *Descartes' Error: Emotion, Reason, and the Human Brain: Antonio Damasio: (First)*. Grosset/Putnam.

Damasio, A. (2000). *The Feeling of What Happens: Body and Emotion in the Making of Consciousness*. Harcourt Inc.

Elias, N., Dunning, Eric, Goudsblom, Johan, & Mennell, Stephen. (2000). *The Civilizing Process: Sociogenetic and Psychogenetic Investigations* (Revised edition). Blackwell Publishers Inc.

Friston, K., & Kiebel, S. (2009). Predictive Coding under the Free-Energy Principle. *Philosophical Transactions of the Royal Society B: Biological Sciences*, 364(1521), 1211–1221. https://doi.org/10.1098/RSTB.2008.0300

Gallagher, S. (2006). *How the Body Shapes the Mind (Paperback)*. Clarendon Press. https://books.google.co.nz/books?hl=en&lr=&id=1FuOy1jPK3UC&oi=fnd&pg=PT3&dq=shaun+gallagher&ots=0lTmLuLt9E&sig=HMkcorCXKTugejbQf0_fMVYbxdc&redir_esc=y#v=onepage&q=shaun+gallagher&f=false

Gladwell, M. (2001). *The Tipping Point: How Little Things make a Big Difference* (2nd edition). Abacus.

Goffman, E. (1980). *The Presentation of Self in Everyday Life (Reprinted)*. Penguin.

Gould, S. J. (2010). *The Panda's Thumb: More Reflections in Natural History (Kindle)*. W.W. Norton and Company. https://www.amazon.com/Pandas-Thumb-Reflections-Natural-History-ebook/dp/B004CRSN5Q/ref=sr_1_6?dib=eyJ2IjoiMSJ9.9bK9Q6lPIp5CLS6T_aI-VbTfMvDKcLs5DkmUfmf1pBHxBgkNRp0jieJOLogwq0p9nrPvfa3x_4pEp0XuokCeMUBBr8jHeCjgCQ1W6sKKcmKVsUY1PP0d5WWdS0agRNlbkJRuf-Y81Jvid4h3LkJagW_byAM3DeukEyLdPPJvPrnDE4Mu3xiryggXkBffQZRNGPCH4xERvNesCriLVijnd_U9Rk-xQI4gqbDckkajI-RTvidi2oozu0ZUEWXg8LEv4NMO_JbBpIREKIJ4B-AjVWXb0do8HueTPkvqSvv7pHI.owsfHw579LojQkXunkF4AWW_fQSY5iEMZK2_zMLsecs&dib_tag=se&qid=1719220317&refinements=p_27%3AStephen+Jay+Gould&s=books&sr=1-6

Gunderson, L. H., & Holling, C. S. (2002). *Panarchy: Understanding Transformations in Human and Natural Systems* (1st edition). Island Press.

Kant, I. (1781). The Critique of Pure Reason. http://www.gutenberg.org/ebooks/4280

Louie, A. H. (2010). Robert Rosen's Anticipatory Systems. *Foresight*, 12(3), 18–29. https://doi.org/10.1108/14636681011049848

Maslow, A. (1943). A Theory of Human Motivation. *Psychological Review*, 50(13), 370–396. https://doi.org/10.1037/h0054346

Maturana, H. (2002). Autopoiesis, Structural Coupling and Cognition: A History of these and Other Notions in the Biology of Cognition. *Cybernetics and Human Knowing*, 9(3), 5–34.

Maturana, H., & Varela, F. J. (1998). *The Tree of Knowledge*. Shambhala Publications.

Michels, R. (1966). *Political Parties: A Sociological Study of the Oligarchical Tendencies of Modern Democracy (Grapevine India)*. Free Press. https://www.google.com/search?gs_ssp=eJzj4tTP1TcwyinLqjBg9FIoyk9KLSpRyM1MzkjNKVYoyM_JLMlMTsxRKEgsKslMLQYAXZQQLA&q=robert+michels+political+parties&oq=roebertmichels+&gs_lcrp=EgZjaHJvbWUqCQgCEC4YDRiABDIGCAAQRRg5MgkIARAAGA0YgAQyCQgCEC4YDRiABDIJCAMQABgNYgAQBgNGIAEMgkIBBAAGA0YgAQyCQgFEAAYDRiABDIJCAYQLhgNGIAEMgkIBxAAGA0YgAQyCQgIEAAYDRiABDIJCAkQLhgNGIAE0gEJMTMwNDNqMGo3qAIAsAIA&sourceid=chrome&ie=UTF-8

New King James Bible. (2018). *NKJV, Value Thinline Bible, Large Print, Leathersoft, Charcoal, Red Letter Edition, Comfort Print: Holy Bible, New King James Version: Thomas Nelson: 9780718075583: Amazon.com: Books*. Thomas Nelson. https://www.amazon.com/Value-Thinline-Leathersoft-Letter-Comfort/dp/0718075587/ref=sr_1_5?crid=303R28AC58SWC&dib=eyJ2IjoiMSJ9.cr44xpQri8LoxWZn5uGvOeTy4dWN0X_ecjjZf0kuMn18iarBwcySdQPZdtzq5co_Th41JANObZsYlkreEG3Ok2GDbgTpAFaNbrV2Ik-cvEgJoP60zOndllWIO6wouyzrWFIw5KfWA9Pm6zthCjZbBVEwwDHupDSE8vokf6-aCtKdwT1SQY_fP-MTLIGVdR6a4udOz71GrGz-SKWPVYjjeqzzwMCjTkgtmIkonGP2lec.

iMoDHrx7Y4ysjB_J5Iu4Z-O1C4QZcKdKhhQ6Zgkfko8&dib_tag=se&keywords=
new+king+james+bible&qid=1721521493&s=books&sprefix=new+king+james+
bibl%2Cstripbooks-intl-ship%2C339&sr=1-5

Rosen, R. (2005). *Life Itself: A Comprehensive Inquiry into the Nature, Origin, and Fabrication of Life.* Columbia University Press.

Stacey, R. D. (1996). *Complexity and Creativity in Organisations.* Berrett-Koehler Publishers.

Stacey, R. D. (2011). *Strategic Management and Organisational Dynamics: The Challenge of Complexity.* Prentice Hall.

Tainter, J. (2007). *The Collapse of Complex Societies* (17th print). Cambridge University Press.

Thompson, E. (2007). *Mind in Life.* Belknap Press.

Varela, F. J., Thompson, E., & Rosch, E. (1993). *The Embodied Mind: Cognitive Science and Human Experience.* Massachusetts Institute of Technology.

Wilber, K. (2000). *Integral Psychology: Consciousness, Spirit, Psychology, Therapy.* Shambhala. http://www.amazon.com/Integral-Psychology-Consciousness-Spirit-Therapy/dp/1570625549

Wilber, K. (2007a). *A Brief History of Everything.* Shambhala Publications. http://books.google.com/books?id=c9shMX7HLY0C&pgis=1

Wilber, K. (2007b). *Integral Spirituality: A Startling New Role for Religion in the Modern and Postmodern World* (Vol. 2007). Shambhala Publications. http://books.google.com/books?id=n-92sivPE2sC&pgis=1

Chapter 4

Human Systems

Introduction

Human beings have evolved a sophisticated brain over millions of years that enables us to link socially far more than any other creatures on earth. All the inherent tensions that set off our evolution remain with us as we struggle to understand ourselves and the lives we create. This chapter is the first of three investigating human systems. We are still only exploring how a single human functions. Later chapters will discuss what happens as humans interact socially. As in previous chapters, we first present relevant concepts to understand life at this level. We begin by looking at how the brain operates and how that impacts how we behave.

The next section covers layers of the brain. We can accurately discuss layers of brain functions but since the brain is so highly interconnected, it is problematic to link specific brain areas to specific functions. Light shines from a lightbulb when we flick the switch, hiding the massive infrastructure required for the light to appear. In the same way, one small part of the brain may seem to control a function, but it is only the trigger set off by other brain functions. Another analogy might be to say that the spark of a spark plug is what makes a car move. While the spark is necessary and sets off the processes that move the car, without a spark plug, without the battery that supplies the charge, the engine block that contains the explosion, the fuel that is injected, or the fuel pump that moves the petrol, and so on, the car does not move. Saying that the amygdala controls anger, for example, is equally problematic. Keep this in mind as you read on. What follows is highly simplified but provides a helpful overview.

The Layers of the Brain

Life evolved from simple forms that developed into increasingly complex layers. This is also true of our brain. The brains of our earliest minded ancestors were basic and automatic. In the centre and at the bottom of our brain is the brainstem, which is sometimes known as the reptile or lizard brain

DOI: 10.4324/9781003533641-4

because reptiles only have a brainstem for their brain. This contains the parts that will later evolve and expand into higher functions but cannot be activated as they are in a human brain.

The brainstem controls basic living functions like breathing, heartbeat, and blood pressure. Our brainstem is markedly different from a reptile's brain, particularly because it connects to all the other parts of the human brain that evolved later. Rather than descending from reptiles, both reptiles and humans actually descend from a common fish ancestor. Mammals are also not descended from reptiles.

The fight/flight response arises from the brainstem. When a reptile senses that its life is in danger, it triggers an immediate, automatic, instinctual survival response of running away or standing and fighting. When we experience any situation, the first filter asks, "Is this a life-threatening event?" If it believes it is, immediate action must be taken from the brainstem. If not deemed to be threatening, the signals from the event can move on for further processing. The fight/flight response triggers adrenaline preparing the body for intense physical activity.

There is an even more primitive response often added to fight and flight: and that is freeze. The body slows so the creature appears dead and does not bleed as much if wounded. The brainstem allows the creature to know if it is safe or unsafe.

As creatures continued to adapt, a brainstem eventually became insufficient to ensure survival and a new layer emerged from the brainstem, called the limbic system. Mammals have a limbic system that gives them the ability to feel emotions. Emotions are generally brief and changeable, allowing us to feel whether something is pleasant or unpleasant. We move towards whatever feels pleasant and away from whatever feels unpleasant or painful. This gives far more flexibility to respond to the environment compared to a lizard. Antonio Damasio writes that feelings arose before emotions.[1] They are related more to homeostasis, the basics of keeping us alive. Feelings include hunger and thirst, pleasure and pain. They are triggered when the body needs to act to survive. As they became more sophisticated, emotions emerged.

Damasio further states that emotions arise in the brain as a response to the state of the body. Body and emotion continuously impact each other. If the fight/flight response is triggered, the amygdala in the limbic system that is involved in anger and fear is generally also triggered.

The thinking level next emerged in the pre-frontal cortex, allowing us to imagine possible futures and apply logical principles to make better decisions. The pre-frontal cortex is far more developed in humans than in other living creatures.

All these skills enable the next level of social skills. Empathy arises at this level. We can learn to apply a myriad of social rules that control how we act in the presence of others.

In a human, the forehead goes straight up from the eyebrows to create space for the large pre-frontal cortex. In a chimpanzee there is no forehead. Figure 4.1 shows how chimpanzee heads slope back at quite an angle because their pre-frontal cortex is much smaller. Figure 4.2 fits these levels into the Dynamics of Life diagram.

The brainstem is like a cottage built for a small family. Over time, that family grew larger, so new buildings were added to the original cottage (limbic system). Many more people came, but they all still only had one

Figure 4.1 A side view of a chimpanzee.   iStock/duncan1890.

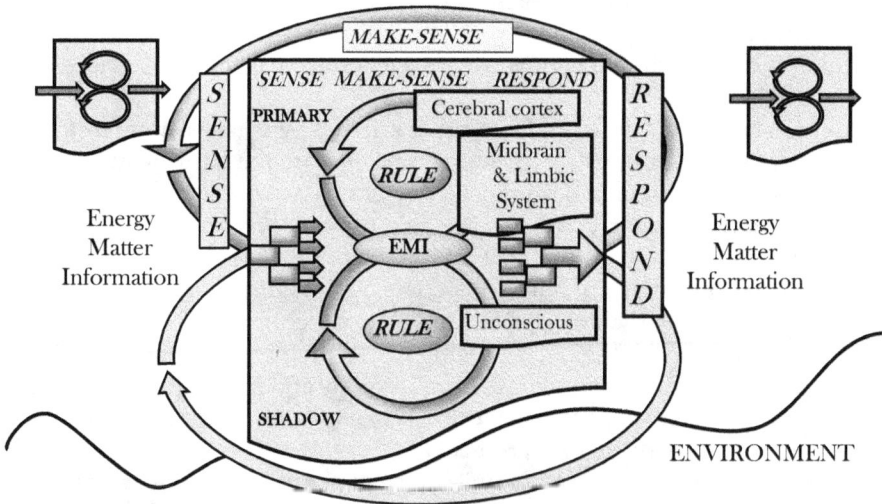

Figure 4.2 A human being as represented by the model. The limbic system and midbrain are combined into the coordinator position.

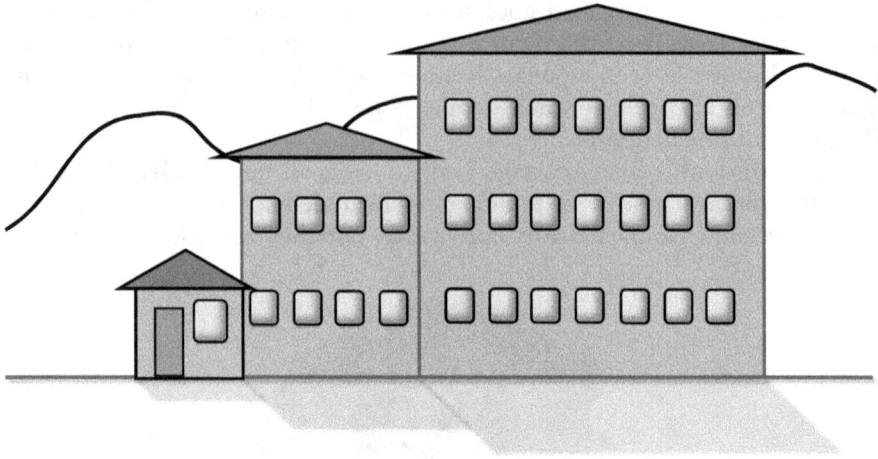

Figure 4.3 The small cottage to the left is like the brainstem, the middle building is like the limbic system and the large building is like the neocortex.

cottage door through which to come and go. The family grew yet again. An even greater building was added to extend what was already built (the prefrontal cortex). Again, there was still only the one door for everyone to come and go through, as shown in Figure 4.3.

There is room for some retrofitting. Electricity and phone lines might be added to the original cottage, but there are limits to how much renovation is possible. As we evolved emotions, and later thinking, all previous structures needed to remain functional. Each new level was built on and relied on previous levels. As always, while simplifying the brain down to three levels is useful, it is a gross simplification. When one level is triggered, messages generally alert all other levels.

Human beings are different from other animals. We have a comparatively large brain for our size, so we give birth early before the baby grows too big to come out of the womb. This means our brains are not as fully developed as other creatures at birth. Horses are able to walk just an hour or so after birth. At birth, we have about 100 billion nerve cells, about the same as we will ever have, but they are only 15% connected. Human brains continue to develop until about the age of 25. Our neurons connect to suit our living environment. Any child is born capable of learning any language, but they will only hear one language, or at most several, and so the brain cells that could have been activated to learn other languages are pruned out by a lack of use, leaving only those that are needed.

If we have a supportive and caring upbringing our brain connects in ways that support openness, trust, honesty, and cooperation. If we have a dysfunctional environment our brain connects for defensiveness, distrust, and hostility. Our brain grows in stages through to maturity. Each new level is activated in sequence. If we experience trauma, the sequence of development is disrupted. Our brains are far more plastic than we previously thought. We can repair incorrectly wired neural growth, but it is like taking a detour on a road. We still get there, but the road is longer and harder. Sometimes the damage is too great to remedy.

Red Brain and Green Brain

Bruce Perry combines the brainstem and limbic system into the *red brain* and calls the pre-frontal cortex the *green brain*.[2] In some versions, he uses the red brain for the brainstem and the yellow brain for the limbic system. The red brain is more primitive, and its focus is ME NOW. Since survival is at stake, the creature focuses on itself rather than others, and on the immediate moment. The fight/flight response is measured in seconds, while emotions generally range from seconds to minutes. Since the fight/flight response is automatic, it can be sparked easily and instantaneously. That works very well in the jungle or on the savannah, but not so well down on Main Street.

The red brain is established on habit patterns. When we repeat something that seemed to work, a pleasurable squirt of dopamine is sent to the basal ganglia in the base of the brain. This makes the response more likely next time, until a habit is formed. Tying shoelaces was difficult when we first tried, but after sufficient repetition, an automatic habit pattern formed in the brain. The brain forms habit patterns to make things simpler like pressing a key on a computer that starts a pre-set software program. We do not have to know what happens in the computer, just which button to press.

When an aeroplane flies in a highly predictable environment, the pilot can turn on the autopilot, which operates from the rules written into the software. It gives the pilot a break to concentrate on other aspects of the flight. Habit patterns are bio-economically cheap, so the brain uses an autopilot habit pattern by default where it deems it sufficient.

The more recently evolved green brain focuses on US FUTURE, as seen in Figure 4.4. A person might be aggravating me. My red brain feels like hitting them, but my green brain thinks about the arrest, the trial, the job loss, the family struggle, and the prison term, and chooses another option. A significant part of the function of the green brain is inhibiting inappropriate red brain urges. We build the social skill of empathy in our green brain, becoming aware of how other people might experience a situation.

Daniel Kahneman makes the same point when he writes of System I and System II. System I functions like the red brain. It is the impulsive, automatic, and intuitive brain. By contrast, System II is like the thoughtful, deliberate, calculating green brain.[3]

Bruce Perry then writes of two types of thinking in the green brain: concentrated or relaxed, which links to Iain McGilchrist's work on the left and right brain.[4] Concentrated thinking on known tasks tends to occur in the left

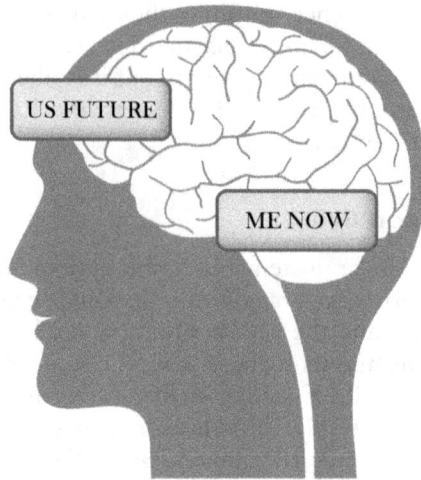

Figure 4.4 The ME NOW response comes from the more primitive red brain and the US FUTURE comes from the green brain.   Adapted from iStock. com/archivector.

brain, which controls the right side of the body. If we fix a car, calculate our tax, or read a technical book, focused thinking is perfect. If we face a situation we have not previously encountered or have a more creative task, then moving into a more relaxed state activates the right brain, which has a more all-encompassing capacity.

I am sure you remember struggling with a task you just couldn't work out. You took a break, went for a walk, watched a video, had a sleep or whatever, and, out of nowhere, the answer suddenly came to you. You first used your left brain, which could not supply the answer; when you were calm enough, however, the right brain re-activated, and the solution appeared simple. Techniques such as yoga, tai chi (my favourite), meditation and relaxation, or simply time by a river or reading a relaxing book all help us to reconnect to our whole selves and activate our calm brain.

Our brain is most fully activated when we are in a relaxed state. People often say we should follow our heart and mistake that for meaning we should follow our emotions. To follow one's heart is to be fully aligned and use our whole brain to make the most of our capacities.

As we become tense, worried, or feel overwhelmed, we lose our relaxed brain's capacity and drop to the focused brain. If we are still overwhelmed, we revert to emotion and, in extreme cases, to pure physical instinct. Alcohol and other substances exacerbate the regression. When you think of a drunk, you think of an angry drunk, a happy drunk, or a sad drunk. The thinking capacity has gone and whatever emotion is on the surface is expressed.

The human brain must cope with an extremely wide range of circumstances. It does this by running two systems in parallel. The red brain is suited to more immediate situations, especially emergencies. The green brain is suited to situations where we need to consider our options more carefully. While running parallel systems enables the brain to cope with a wide range of possible circumstances, it creates the dilemma of deciding which system to use in each circumstance.

We can be tempted to think the green brain is good and the red brain is bad, but both are vital to our survival and thriving. If I step onto the street in front of a car speeding towards me, my red brain will get me to move immediately to get me out of danger. We cannot use the green brain without activating the red brain. Problems particularly arise when the red brain takes charge in situations where the slower green brain would have led to a smarter decision. Through practice, we can improve our capacity to STOP and THINK so we use our whole brain to make sense of our experience.

Our identity is that which is conserved in the process of living. A wild animal's sense of identity is its body that it seeks to conserve. Human identity includes the body, but also adds your name, beliefs, culture, personality, emotions, thoughts, social reputation, physical possessions, and more.

The fight/flight mechanism is triggered when we sense a threat to our well-being. Today, however, our fight/flight mechanism is triggered for events that are not life-threatening. If my name is attacked, this feels like an attack on my body. When I see a car park as I drive to the supermarket, it becomes "my car park", a part of me as much as my arm or leg. When someone takes "my park", we can feel enraged. We might feel upset and angry, but we are not about to die.

If you come across a car accident with multiple victims, the red brain temptation is to rush in and help straight away. You are drawn to the person screaming in pain, but a more thoughtful green approach will reveal that the person quietly falling unconscious behind them is in far more danger. There might be hidden electric cables or the risk of a petrol explosion. In that situation, the counterintuitive slower, more conscious, deliberate approach will be the most beneficial.

The brain has a store of habit patterns it prefers built over a lifetime because they are easy and use less energy. We do not have to think of our heartbeat, blood pressure, and thousands of other body processes. They happen on autopilot. We can stop our emotions from spinning out of control, but we cannot stop them from arising. George Lakoff observes that 98% or more of our thinking is habitual. You will recognise the internal chatter that continues mostly unnoticed in our heads all day. Habit patterns are extremely useful but sometimes old habit patterns that may have made sense 30 years ago, or did not even make sense then, just make the situation worse.

The brain must overcome the problem that the red brain operates much faster than the green because the green brain considers so much more information before reaching a conclusion. As soon as the red brain decides its identity is under threat it tries to shut the green brain down because it will slow it up in the perceived emergency. Within the green brain is a part called the dorsolateral pre-frontal cortex that Kathryn Berkett calls "Bob", which sends a STOP AND THINK message before the red brain takes over and creates space for the green brain to catch up. You can practise using Bob until Bob becomes a new habit, avoiding the red brain taking over.

The red brain and the green brain are like people in a two-seater car. Only one can be the driver, and since there is always a habit pattern waiting to be activated, the red brain is already in the driver's seat. Unless the green brain uses Bob, or finds a way to shift the red brain from the driver's seat, the red brain will put its foot to the floor and take off. Benjamin Libet[5] looked at free will and decided that we actually have *free won't*. We have the power to say no to the red brain, but unless we actively choose the green brain over the red brain, the red brain will act. Think of how you experience the tension between the red and the green brain vying for control over your actions. Think of times when the red brain took control. How did that work out? Then, think of times the green brain took control. How did that work out?

We now move away from exploring the brain and its function to look more closely at the meaning-making process. Meaning-making is central to human life because when we find meaning, we know how to act.

Meaning-Making

Just as we digest food, we digest our experiences to generate emotions and thoughts, so we know what to do. We absorb energy from our interactions to make sense of our experiences and formulate the best response. There are several concepts to explore before learning tools to cope with anger and violence. Information shows us the patterns, but knowledge gives meaning.

Metaphors

When we take one concept, idea, image, sound, thought, object, or whatever and link it to another, we create a metaphor. George Lakoff tells us that a conceptual metaphor is a metaphor in which "one idea is understood in terms of another". The idea of a *stormy meeting*, for example, links a group of people in a room having a conflicted meeting to stormy weather. He even says that whenever we form a metaphor, we do it by physically connecting the brain cells associated with the metaphor. That means our brains literally grow differently according to the metaphors we choose and how we link them.

We use already known concepts to form metaphors that can describe something not yet known. While in Australia I came across a *pademelon*. It was a small kangaroo, only about 50 centimetres high, as pictured in Figure 4.5. By understanding the concepts "small" and "kangaroo", I was able to give you an understanding of something you did not know (unless you are Australian!).

Figure 4.5 A pademelon.   iStock.com/tracielouise.

Once we have one metaphor, it can be linked to other metaphors to create a connected network of coherent ideas. Metaphors form the foundation of language, connecting us to the world through the patterns we find. Metaphors structure language and language structures metaphors.

Our first metaphor is inside and outside. A newborn baby perceives the world as one big undifferentiated mass, just a big jumble of sights, sounds, tastes, smells, and touch. It must be so confusing. The baby will eventually recognise that its experience of its hand is different from its experience of a cot, toy, door, and mother. The hand can be perceived as an object out in the world like the cot and toy; unlike the cot and the toy, however, the hand has internal sensation. The baby can feel the muscles move, feel it bang against the side of the cot, feel cold or warm. The baby has a burgeoning sense of control over it. It will eventually recognise that its foot, nose, and stomach are like its hand. The baby learns it has a body separate from things like the cot, toy, door, and mother. Now inside and outside exist. This is the birth of duality. From now on, the world is fragmented and broken into separate parts.

Forming the concept of what we know as mother is no mean feat for a baby. The baby must recognise that a certain living being who looks very different when viewed from different angles, sometimes close and sometimes far, from the front, from the back, often wearing different clothing, having hair arranged in different ways, are all different expressions of the same concept of mother. When the baby is held and comforted by the mother, especially when feeding, it feels fused, making it difficult to recognise where the boundary between the two lies. The baby would most usually tag the mother as safe, warm, and protective. She becomes an enduring concept rather than just the various sensations perceived when the mother is present. Our whole world is thus formed by concepts, which are mental constructions and not the various sensations we have perceived. As more and more concepts are developed, they interact with each other in complex ways, forming patterns and patterns of patterns. Read a small piece from a newspaper, magazine,

Facebook message, or whatever, and look for the metaphors. Notice how often they appear and how they hold up the language.

Our individual networks of metaphors need to be constrained and aligned with other people's metaphors so we can communicate. Our family and community provide the conceptual patterns of language and culture that shape the neural pathways in our brains. My concept of "mother" must be sufficiently like your concept of "mother" so we can both understand the same thing when it is referred to. Shared ritualised behaviours become enculturated. Each culture has its own shared understandings and metaphors to describe its world. Each concept is tagged with an emotional state, so mother keeping me warm and safe is pleasurable. Pooey nappies are uncomfortable, and hot objects are threatening and painful. In this way, a child develops a cognitive map to "map" its cognitive world.

I remember walking down the road many years ago, watching a mother and small boy walking in front of me. The little boy suddenly jumped in the air and waved his arms and legs wildly about before coming down to the ground again. I suddenly realised this was not "just playing" or moving randomly. He was making connections. He had crafted a precise scientific experiment to learn what a particular set of movements felt like internally, what he could do with his body, and how it impacted the external world. It was all being linked as metaphors and mapped in his mind, telling him more about himself and his world. As he did it, he watched his mother and saw her annoyance, so he mapped his mother's disapproval.

In the same way that we make predictions about our physical environment, we make predictions about our social environment, to know what to expect. Lakoff talks of the metaphor of life as a journey. As we travel from one place to another, we encounter obstacles, find ourselves lost in the dark, reach a downhill stretch, find our way again, and so on.

All languages I have known connect time and space. A long journey takes a long time. A short journey takes a short time. The end can be an ending in time or in place. The future in most cultures is in front of us and the past behind us.

Over time, the baby's cognitive map becomes increasingly complex. The baby links metaphors to make sense of the world. Some babies will connect their mother with safety and security, while others will link her to abandonment, loss, and isolation. The foundation of the map is set by age three and is largely formed by the age of seven. The child forms their map to the best of their ability, but naturally they make mistakes. A child typically assumes that if an adult does something or says something it is correct and absorbs the perception as truth.

A child misperceives events and makes incorrect conclusions about the world. It is like Captain Cook's exploration of New Zealand in 1769. He charted the country as best he could with the limited technology available. While the general shape of New Zealand is immediately recognisable, he made notable errors, charting Banks Peninsula as an island and Stewart Island as a peninsula, as you will see by comparing Figures 4.6a and 4.6b.

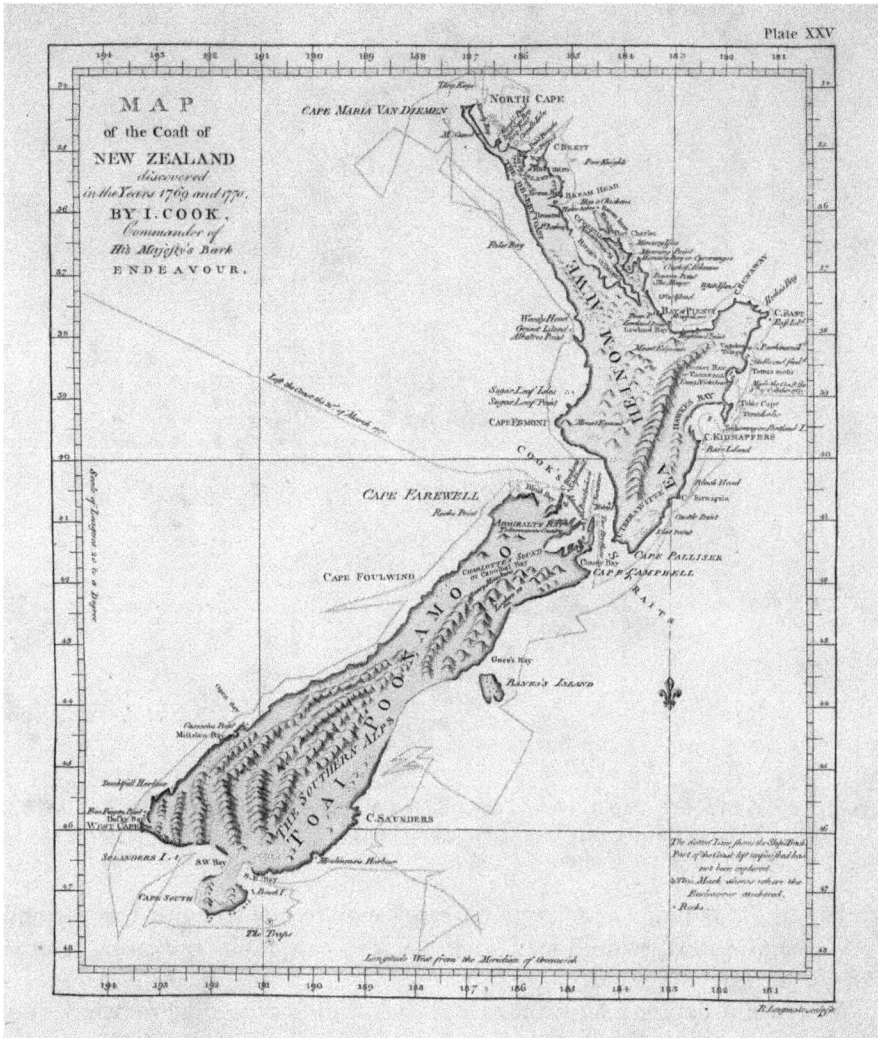

(a)

Figure 4.6a The map of New Zealand as drawn by Captain Cook. (Cook, James, 1728–1779. [Cook, James] 1728–1779: Map of the coast of the New Zealand discovered in the years 1769 and 1770, By I. Cook, Commander of His Majesty's Bark Endeavour. B. Longmate sculpsit. [London, 1773]. Parkinson, Sydney, 1745–1771: A journal of a voyage to the South Seas, in his Majesty's ship, "The Endeavour". Faithfully transcribed from the papers of the late Sydney Parkinson. London; Printed for Charles Dilly, in the Poultry, and James Phillips, in the George-Yard, 1784. Ref: PUBL-0037-25. Alexander Turnbull Library, Wellington, New Zealand. /records/22751427).

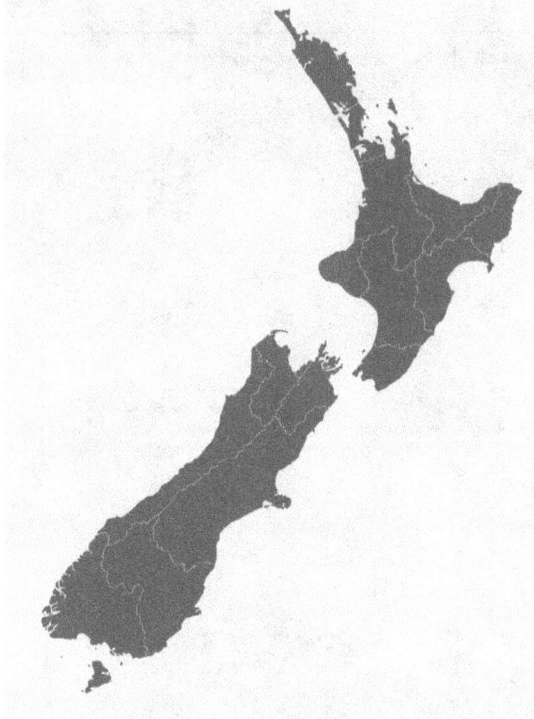

(b)

Figure 4.6b A modern map of New Zealand for comparison.   iStock.com/rambo182,
https://www.istockphoto.com/vector/new-zeland-gm158424515-
13143171.

In the same way that using Captain Cook's map to navigate our way around New Zealand today would lead to disaster, so can adults operating from a map formed in childhood.

We saw in Chapter 2 how animals evolved values according to behaviours that helped them survive. Light, openness, and being higher kept them safe in the physical realm. When the cognitive realm evolved, instead of starting over, we simply copied the physical values to the cognitive realm. What was deemed safe at the physical level became good at the cognitive level.

From the biological level, light was valued over dark; thus, at the cognitive level light becomes a metaphor for goodness. Light takes on a spiritual value of purity and darkness becomes evil. Being open is preferred to being hidden. A link is made between a person who hides in the shadows to avoid being seen and a person who stays quiet, not speaking up and avoiding being noticed as also being hidden.

To do something behind someone's back means they cannot see what is done, but it generalises to include situations where information is withheld from someone. They were fooled by the information to which they were not privy. A baby feels warm in its mother's arms. We talk of a caring, supportive person as having a warm heart, while someone with a cold heart is callous and uncaring.

Up is seen as progress and suggests improvement and growth. Something higher is more venerated. There are strong links between *up* and *more*. As I pour more liquid into a cup, the level goes up. To go down or backwards is to deteriorate.

The body is the foundation of life and so the body also becomes a key metaphor. Rivers have mouths, trees have trunks and limbs, lakes have arms, aeroplanes have tails and wings, and businesses have head offices and branches.

Our language is filled with military metaphors so that, without recognising it, we keep reinforcing militaristic concepts depicting life as a battlefield filled with conflict and aggression. We talk of the war on drugs, political campaigns, giving it your best shot, losing ground, and fighting an uphill battle. COVID-19 and other pandemics are often presented as an enemy to be defeated. Business is seen as a war against competitors. We speak of aiming for a target, rallying the troops, beating the competition, and making a killing.

The metaphors we use matter because they shape how we see the world and make sense of it. Changing metaphors and changing the way we use language impacts powerfully on how we might influence others or be influenced by them, and on how we shape our sense of identity.[6]

Values and Beliefs

Building the network of metaphors allowed the formation of a coherent way of looking at the world. This network of metaphors forms the foundation of values and beliefs, which become enshrined into the rule set at the level of mind.[7] When we act in alignment with our values, we feel comfortable; when we fail, we feel guilt or shame. How I believe the world to be, what I choose to value, and what I reject, determines my actions. If I have strong family values, I will act to protect my family. Strong religious beliefs will guide my actions within the beliefs I follow.

If I believe "I am always right", I will act according to that belief. If people contradict that belief I will react. People may respond to my reaction in ways that further challenge my belief. In this way, that which we cannot integrate into our world returns to us. We might call it karma.

When the world contradicts our beliefs, we can change them by revising our map, or we can retain our map by distorting our beliefs to justify ourselves. A drug addict can justify their actions in terms of the pleasant high, while ignoring the later negative impacts of their choices. An inept worker might blame others rather than acknowledge the truth. A useful question is,

"Do the beliefs and values I hold take me towards the future I seek or further away?" If they take you further away, it may be time to reassess your belief systems.

We are conscious of some beliefs, but we also have values and beliefs that are so deep and normalised that we stop noticing their impact on our lives. Such core beliefs form the foundation of our beliefs and values. Common core beliefs are "I am unworthy", "The world is a dangerous place" and "I am unlovable". Once such beliefs are embedded in our being they can sabotage our efforts to live effectively. These core beliefs then generate aligned beliefs and values.

Our beliefs and values often clash. If you hold the beliefs, "Support my family" and "You should not steal", hearing that your brother stole a car creates a tension as to which value is more important. There are often clashes and tensions between the member level and the coordinating level, or the leader level. Tension between a partner and children or a partner and parents is also common.

Systems Justification Theory

The Justification Hypothesis is a part of Gregg Henriques' Tree of Knowledge concept. At the thinking level, we shape our cognitive mapping to maintain a positive, internally consistent sense of identity. There will be times when there is dissonance between the map we created and the world as it is. Ideally, at this point the cognitive map is changed to align the behaviour with the new reality; often, however, we distort our perception of the world, to avoid having to change the map. The map charts our identity, so a perceived threat to our identity is often experienced as a life-threatening situation.

Self-talk is an internal dialogue that integrates new events into the existing narrative as they arise. You can talk yourself into a new way of understanding and say, "Maybe I expected too much of them" or justify keeping the map the same. Your self-talk might be, "What do they know, they're just jealous?", "They should treat me better", or "They're just incompetent". Justifications typically use denial, minimising, and blaming.

Abuse or violence usually creates dissonance between someone's actions and their view of themselves, so justifications of violence are typical. From experience, 90% or more of people sent to undertake a non-violence programme with me will say during the first meeting, "I am not a violent person". People will formulate an understanding of what violence is, and is not, to fit around their perception of themselves. Justifications for violence I hear range from, "They deserved it for what they did", to "It was an accident" or "She should have known not to push me like that" through to "I am the victim here". There may have been truth in some of these comments, but they are all justifications to manage the sense of self-worth and present an acceptable public face.

We can all be violent or abusive to some degree, either through what we do or through what we fail to do. With all our best intentions we say and do hurtful things to ourselves and others. We are all complicit in unimaginable violence to people in the developing world who suffer and die so we can continue to buy our computers, phones, clothes, and other consumer items.

The justification system is operated by the ego to manage the conflict between the childish desires of the lower mind (or *id*) and the rules of the upper mind (or *superego*). Our lives are in constant tension. Henriques called the id the experiential self, which just absorbs events. The experiential self is unconscious and does not reflect on its experience. Freud saw the experiential self as being ruled by sex and aggression. Henriques talks instead about behavioural investment, as in a creature that balances the expected reward of an action like food, against the likelihood of a threat like a predator.

We have a public and a private face, which are based on thinking and language. The private self is the ego, which includes reflections about ourselves we are willing to accept. It must formulate stories to contain the behaviours emerging from the experiential self. The public self is concerned with how we appear to others and how that impacts our social standing. We wish to be seen as acceptable, trustworthy, and worthy of belonging. Lying or distorting the truth can be used to alter our presentation of ourselves back to ourselves and to others. This can be done either consciously or unconsciously. Children often show naive honesty because they have not yet learned what is acceptable in public and what is not.

Henriques writes of a filter (The Freudian filter) between the experiential self and the private self, where unpleasant experiences are filtered out of consciousness. As we repress experience, we create a justification story for the private self. A second filter (The Rogerian filter) lies between the private and public self as depicted in Figure 4.7. We do not like to be judged as inadequate or bad, so we filter out behaviours that will show us in a bad light. We tend to take credit for the good we do and blame others for our mistakes. Brené Brown told a story,[8] recounting when she dropped a cup of coffee that broke on the floor and made a mess. In an instant, she had formulated a justification allowing herself to blame her husband for the break. He had been playing water polo the night before and came back late so she went to bed later and in the morning needed a second cup of coffee – which broke. Her justification is obviously irrational, but it shows how easily we create irrational justifications to avoid acknowledging our errors.

We wear a social mask shaping our presentation of ourselves to maintain or enhance our social reputation. We share our justification stories with others. Sometimes, we unconsciously agree together to hide part of our shared experiences as an "elephant in the room". We keep family secrets, or we scapegoat an individual to take on the parts of ourselves we are unwilling or unable to integrate.

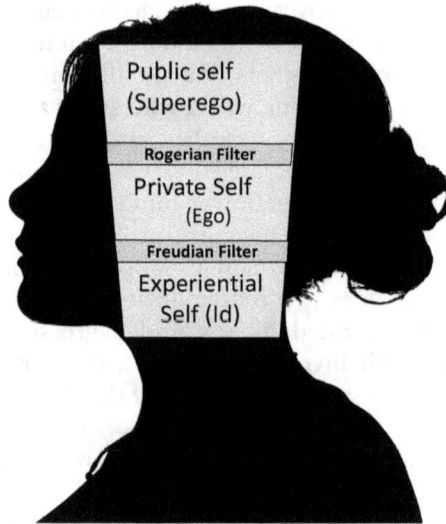

Public self
(Superego)

Rogerian Filter

Private Self
(Ego)

Freudian Filter

Experiential
Self (Id)

Figure 4.7 Gregg Henriques' Updated Tripartite Model.   Reprinted with permission of Gregg Henriques. Woman's head, Gordon Johnson, https://pixabay.com/vectors/woman-profile-silhouette-people-7128718/, Pixabay Content License.

We justify to fit in with the people around us, showing that justification has a large cultural component. Some cultures demand higher levels of compliance or have different standards that will impact on how the justification process operates. Science, religion, and neo-liberal economics are all justification systems that operate across whole societies and nations, forming a cohesive set of agreed ways of looking at life. They all have blind spots that create consequences.

Once you know what to look for, you constantly see and hear justifications around you. Having the courage to openly look at our own justification stories opens a powerful tool for personal development. When we notice others justifying, we can see it as a flaw in the other, or just a recognition of our shared humanity. They are merely doing what we all do to maintain our inner coherence.

Trauma

Traumatic life events interfere with the natural laying down of neural pathways in the brain. The rule set that forms the basis of cognitive mapping is disrupted and connected in unhelpful and destructive ways. It is like a physical map that has been torn up and needs to be fitted back together, or possessing a map of New York when we are in London. What is neutral or even helpful is viewed as a threat, triggering an inappropriate red brain response.

Music playing while trauma is being experienced may be linked so that hearing similar music can trigger the memory of the trauma and bring it back into the present moment. Trust and openness are lost.

Trauma can arise out of a range of distressing events, such as natural disasters, war, or abuse and violence. For others, it is through chronic tension that is not released. To a small baby a parent simply going out of the room could be particularly frightening. Without a concept of time, the baby does not know whether the parent will return. They only know they are gone and the baby feels abandoned.[9] Trauma may arise before birth, such as when the mother drinks alcohol. Everyone responds to trauma in their own way and has unique triggers. Even the best of parents may unintentionally cause a level of trauma for their child.

Trauma and addictions

Addictions often arise as a way of coping with traumatic events. An addiction is a behaviour intended to meet a need, that appears to solve the problem or anxiety in the short term but has significant adverse effects in the long term.[10] Many addictions cause obvious, visible harm. Others are less visible. Some are even sanctioned and rewarded, such as overworking, fitness, overeating, and digital media use.

When we have a problem anxiety commonly arises. If we cannot or choose not to resolve the problem, we sometimes focus on just removing the anxiety to make life bearable. This can be seen in Figure 4.8. Addictions offer short-term relief at the cost of later harm. In choosing the addiction the person now has two problems, which of course means anxiety levels increase, leading to a greater level of addiction being needed to cover the anxiety. A positive feedback loop has been established making the situation even worse.

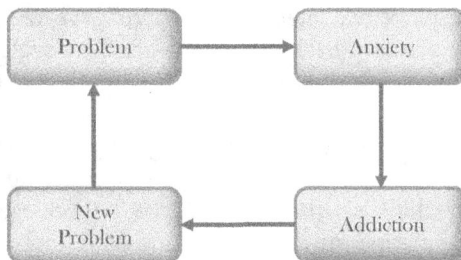

Figure 4.8 The cycle of addiction. Problems generate anxiety. Instead of solving the problem, an addiction is used to reduce the anxiety, but that creates more problems.

Deception

Living creatures came to realise they could intentionally deceive other living systems so they would make errors. Deception might help avoid detection or make prey easier to catch. Camouflage is an attempt to blur the boundary between the creature and its environment to make it less visible. Octopuses eject a black ink that looks like an octopus to confuse and distract predators. In mythology, the Wooden Horse of Troy was built to appear as though it was a gift left by an army accepting defeat, whereas the horse was filled with warriors, who emerged once the horse was pulled inside the city.

Telling lies in human communication sends incorrect information usually said to avoid something undesirable being revealed. We lie directly, through untruths, or deceive by omission. While deceiving others might generate benefits for a person, being caught deceiving will receive condemnation because of its corrosive effect on trust and group cohesion.

There are times when lies are acceptable or even rewarded. In a financial transaction, it is understood that one does not divulge facts like your top price or the lowest price you will accept. At other times, we tell white lies to avoid hurting someone's feelings. We think we teach children to be honest and not tell lies, when in fact we teach them by our actions where and when lying is acceptable or even expected.

Deception can lead to an evolutionary war in which the prey or victim develops more sophisticated forms of deception, the predator evolves increasingly effective ways of detecting deception leading to a war of ratcheted-up deception and detection.

Acknowledging the Dark Side

Star Wars presented a world with a sharp and clear boundary between the light and the dark. While it is mythologically powerful, we are all a mix of both. A step on the journey of living beyond violence is the acceptance of our capacity for violence and an acknowledgement of abusive or violent practices. As long as we place the enemy "out there", we will not find peace in ourselves. For every primary cycle, there is a shadow cycle.[11] They co-create each other and recursively and inextricably arise both within us and between us and the world we live in.

Zak Stein talks of the three stages of pre-tragic, tragic, and post-tragic.[12] The pre-tragic is the ever-hopeful youth who has not come up against the harsh realities of life. Everything seems possible. It is a wonderful, if deluded, life stage that can rekindle hope for a better future. Many movies depict a young person bringing a rigid, defeated, and worn-down older person back to life.

The next stage is the tragic stage, where we become trapped in pain and suffering and lose the ability to see our situation accurately. The only way to navigate to the post-tragic stage is through the tragic. The cause of our suffering is usually placed outside ourselves. We must embrace the pain and live through it. There will be irretrievable loss.

As hard as it is, the way forward is the way through. One of the central concepts of my first book, *When the Dragon Stirs*, recognises that *The Dragon is the Pathway to Peace*. Zak Stein cites blues singers as a group who have entered their pain in a way that enables them to move forward. They find a place of peace, of coming to a point of oneness in themselves that includes the shadow with all the heartache and evil in the world.

There are many things in the world out there that are not as we would like them to be, and it is right that we should stand up and have our say, and resist and protest. We should, however, best do it with an open mind as to how we might be misinterpreting the situation to suit our own perceived needs. We can easily miss how we might be complicit in what we perceive as evil. Since we are all connected and no part of the universe can stand alone, if there is evil in the world, it is in us too. I remember reading of protests in Germany about the pollution caused by coal-fired power plants and realising that the protesters travelled to the protest in their oil-burning vehicles.

It is virtually impossible to live and make a meaningful contribution to life in the modern world without participating in the pollution and destruction of the environment. I could ride a bicycle to stop burning oil, but how much oil was burned in making and maintaining the bicycle. Electric vehicles use rare earth metals and slave labour.

The reality is that we each find a level of complicity we are comfortable with, just as we find the level of conflict and risk we are prepared to live with. We could reduce our highway speed limits, but in fact, we are prepared to accept a level of complicity to make life bearably comfortable.

We have an enormous capacity to deceive ourselves and others, particularly if our lives and livelihoods depend on remaining oblivious to what is happening. People living next to Nazi death camps, working for cigarette companies, and multinational companies using virtual slave labour to produce cheap consumer goods for the West all knew what they were doing but chose to continue. We all do it in our own way.

Thich Nhat Hanh worked helping villagers in Vietnam during what the Vietnamese call the American War. He recognised that the murderous actions of the Americans also sat within himself and that he had to come to terms with his anger and resentment that arose as a response to American atrocities.

Hannah Arendt wrote of the "banality of evil" after witnessing the Nuremberg trials following World War II.[13] Men who were otherwise caring gentle people within their family could go to work and orchestrate the murder of thousands of human beings. We should not delude ourselves about our potential for violence towards others. Stanley Milgram conducted experiments that would be banned today, showing that people were willing to give what they believed to be lethal electric shocks, simply because a person of authority commanded them to do so. His other well-known experiment was having students randomly selected to take the role of either guard or prisoner in a fictitious prison environment in a university. The experiment had to be abandoned only a couple of days into the experiment because of the violence the "guards" were prepared to perpetrate on those given the role of prisoner. This might sound negative and scary, but the acknowledgment of the violence in our nature is the turning point, where we can begin healing and changing the behaviours that have held us back.

Truly noticing our dark side requires great courage and insight. We have so many cognitive systems set up to avoid seeing the darker side. It is incredibly uncomfortable. What can you recognise as your own darker side, that you might work towards healing?

Key Points

1 The human brain has four basic layers of functioning: the brain stem linked to the survival function, out of which evolved the limbic system linked to emotions and out of the limbic system, the neocortex linked to thinking and social level.
2 The human brain is only 15% connected at birth and the connections grow to adapt to the environment. The environment is critical to human development, especially in earlier years.
3 The red brain focuses on ME NOW while the green brain focuses on US FUTURE.
4 The red and green brain compete for control. "Bob" in the green brain can be quick enough to stop the red brain from taking control at the wrong time.
5 We use metaphors to understand new things by comparing them to things we know.
6 Shared metaphors form the basis of culture and enable communication.
7 How we view ourselves and our world are enshrined in our beliefs, which shape and guide our decisions.
8 We justify ourselves to avoid having to acknowledge the truth and reconfigure our view of ourselves.
9 We create shared justification stories that create "elephants in the room" we tacitly agree to ignore.
10 Trauma impacts our ability to re-wire the brain in unhelpful ways. Additions are often used to try and cope with addiction.
11 The first step in healing is the acknowledgment of our capacity for violence, whether intentional or not.

Notes

1 See *Feeling and Knowing, Making Minds Conscious* by Antonio Damasio.
2 In reality, because of how interconnected the brain is, it is not an easy task to precisely determine which brain parts are in the green and which are in the red. It may be more helpful to think in terms of brain functions rather than gross anatomical placement.
3 See *Thinking: Fast and Slow* by Daniel Kahneman for more detail.

4 See *The Master and his Emissary* by Iain McGilchrist for more detail.
5 See *Conscious Intention and Brain Activity* by B. Libet and P. Haggard.
6 See *Metaphors We Live By* by George Lakoff and Mark Johnson.
7 See *Maps of Meaning* by Jordan Peterson.
8 https://www.youtube.com/watch?v=RZWf2_2L2v8.
9 See *What Happened to You* by Bruce Perry and Oprah Winfrey.
10 See *When the Body Says No* by Gabor Mate.
11 See *Man and his Symbols* by Carl Jung.
12 https://www.youtube.com/watch?v=BRGU1Q-5sgU.
13 See *Eichmann in Jerusalem* by Hannah Arendt.

Bibliography

Arendt, H. (2006). *Eichmann in Jerusalem (Penguin Classics)*. Penguin Classics. http://www.amazon.com/Eichmann-Jerusalem-Penguin-Classics-Hannah/dp/0143039881

Damasio, A. (1994). *Descartes' Error: Emotion, Reason, and the Human Brain: Antonio Damasio: (First)*. Grosset/Putnam.

Damasio, A. (2000). *The Feeling of What Happens: Body and Emotion in the Making of Consciousness*. Harcourt Inc.

Ettinger, D., & Jehiel, P. (2010). A Theory of Deception. *American Economic Journal: Microeconomics*, 2(1), 1–20. https://doi.org/10.1257/mic.2.1.1

Feldman Barrett, L. (2017). *How Emotions are Made: The Secret Life of the Brain*. Pan Books. https://www.amazon.com/How-Emotions-Are-Made-Thinking-ebook/dp/B06WLMGNRX?ref_=ast_author_dp

Haggard, P., & Libet, B. (2001). Conscious Intention and Brain Activity. *Journal of Consciousness Studies*, 8(11), 47–64.

Henriques, G. (2011). The Problem of Psychology. *A New Unified Theory of Psychology*, 29–42. https://doi.org/10.1007/978-1-4614-0058-5_2

Henriques, G. (2022). *A New Synthesis for Solving the Problem of Psychology: Addressing the Enlightenment Gap*. Palgrave Macmillan. https://www.amazon.com/Synthesis-Solving-Problem-Psychology-Enlightenment-ebook/dp/B0BPQFYLTG/ref=sr_1_1?crid=2K8ZHMGHJLMH&keywords=gregg+henriques&qid=1677049032&sprefix=gregg+henriques%2Caps%2C480&sr=8-1

Jung, C. (2010). *Answer to Job*. Princeton University Press.

Jung, C. (2014). *The Archetypes and the Unconscious (Collected Works of C.G Jung)* (2nd edition). Routledge.

Jung, C. G. (1968). *Man and His Symbols*. Dell. http://www.amazon.com/Man-Symbols-Carl-Gustav-Jung/dp/0440351839

Kahneman, D. (2015). Thinking, Fast and Slow. In *College Music Symposium* (First pape, Vol. 55). Farrar, Strauss & Giroux. https://doi.org/10.18177/sym.2015.55.ca.10990

van der Kolk, B. (2015). *The Body Keeps the Score: Brain, Mind and Body in the Healing of Trauma*. Penguin.

Lakoff, G., & Johnson, M. (1980). *Metaphors We Live By*. University of Chicago Press.

Mate, G. (2003). *When the Body Says No*. Wiley. https://books.google.co.nz/books?hl=en&lr=&id=8hjoyCFTu6IC&oi=fnd&pg=PA169&dq=GABor+mATE&ots=EWMP7cLPnf&sig=IFT1ddP6d1vuuDkRkXaaVqKD9cA&redir_esc=y#v=onepage&q=GABormATE&f=false

Mcgilchrist, I. (2009). *The Master and His Emissary: The Divided Brain and the Making of the Western World*. Yale University Press. https://www.amazon.com/Master-His-Emissary-Divided-Western/dp/030014878X/ref=tmm_hrd_swatch_0?_encoding=UTF8&qid=&sr=

Mcgilchrist, I. (2021). *The Matter with Things: Our Brains, our Delusions and the Unmaking of the World*. Perspectiva Press. https://www.amazon.com/Matter-Things-Brains-Delusions-Unmaking-ebook/dp/B09KY5B3QL

Milgram, S. (2017). *Obedience to Authority: The Experiment That Challenged Human Nature* (Reprint Edition). Harper Perennial.

Perry, B., & Szalavitz, M. (2017). *The Boy Who Was Raised as a Dog: And Other Stories from a Child Psychiatrist's Notebook: What Traumatized Children Can Teach Us about Loss, Love, and Healing*. Basic Books. https://www.amazon.com/Boy-Who-Raised-Psychiatrists-Notebook-What-ebook/dp/B06XS49X4D/ref=sr_1_1?crid=2H VIJQHYHEDFK&keywords=bruce+perry&qid=1677051943&sprefix=bruce+perry%2Caps%2C481&sr=8-1

Perry, B., & Winfrey, O. (2021). *What Happened to You: Conversations on Trauma, Resilience and Healing*. Flatiron Books.

Peterson, J. B. (1999). *Maps of Meaning: The Architecture of Belief*. Routledge.

Chapter 5

Changing Behaviour

Introduction

With an overview of how the brain and body function, we can move on to explore ways to change behaviour patterns to live more effectively and produce better outcomes. There are three main approaches to changing individual behaviour.

The first is emotional regulation. Emotion only tells us how we feel in the moment, and not what we *should* do. The higher our level of emotion, the worse our thinking. When a person is too driven by their emotion, they become overwhelmed in the moment and act rashly creating unhelpful outcomes.

The second approach is to develop awareness. Nothing will change for an alcoholic harming themselves and others until there is an awareness and acceptance of the harm being caused. Often, the first step of healing is just noticing. Once we are aware, we can choose to act differently and learn new strategies. When we are mindful of ourselves and our situation, we notice how our habit patterns work both for and against us. We will have a greater understanding of other people and develop empathy.

The third approach is through restructuring beliefs and values. If they are based on negative attitudes, harm will unfold. There are techniques to reprogramme the basic software running the brain to build our sense of well-being and that of others. Our thinking is shaped by our beliefs and values. Changing thinking can change beliefs and values.

Each of these three approaches will be explored, looking at tools and strategies that can be used to build strength. Some techniques focus on one of the approaches while other tools, like Tai Chi, yoga, meditation, and relaxation, are especially powerful because they link all the approaches and all levels of functioning in a coherent manner.

DOI: 10.4324/9781003533641-5

Emotional Well-being

1–10 Anger Scale

The 1–10 scale is a simple scale that rates feelings of anger on a scale from 1, feeling calm and relaxed through to 10, where a person is as angry as they can imagine (Table 5.1). The 1–10 scale could be used for many other emotional states, such as anxiety, depression, pain, or joy. Its simplicity belies its effectiveness. Having used this scale for many years, I am continually amazed that such a simple tool can make such a difference in people's lives. Once people notice their emotional state, they can choose to act.

The scale is often depicted as traffic lights, so 1–4 is green. In the green our ability to remain calm and think clearly helps us cope with most situations. From 5–7 is the orange light. Here our ability to think clearly is still usually adequate, but coping becomes increasingly difficult. Finally, from 8–10 is the red light. Our capacity to think clearly is much reduced and we are likely to revert to fight/flight functioning. The use of alcohol or drugs further reduces our ability to make good decisions. People are often at a higher point on the scale than they realise, so building the habit pattern of regularly monitoring and checking is powerful.

When we are at 4 and recognise that if we do not do something differently, we will continue up the scale to 5, 6, and beyond, it is the ideal time to stop and think about the situation and how to handle it. The next critical number is 6. If we are at 6 and still rising, we have reached our last opportunity to stop and think about what we need to do before our emotions take over and we lose the capacity for rational thought.

We know where we are on the scale by the sensations we feel in our bodies. Typically, when we are at 1–2 we will feel a slow and steady heartbeat, slow and steady breathing, a warm comfortable body temperature, relaxed muscles, and generally little movement. The stomach feels calm and

Table 5.1 The 1:10 scale describing levels of anger

Traffic light	Anger rating	Description
	10	Total rage
(Red)	9	Rage
	8	Angry lost control
	7	Angry and starting to lose it
(Orange)	6	Angry and just holding on
	5	Angry
	4	Annoyed
(Green)	3	Irritable
	2	Mild irritation
	1	Calm, relaxed

comfortable. Our thoughts will be calm and clear. By the time we reach 6, several body signs are typically experienced. Heart rate will be elevated, and breathing will be heavier and faster. For some people, breathing will become shallower and faster. Muscles become tense and the body hotter. Movements are fidgety and there is pacing. People often talk of their stomachs being knotted, or tight, or having butterflies. There are exceptions. Some people feel cold when angry. Some people appear calm on the outside but are seething inside. It is valuable to be aware of our individual bodily responses.

Breathing

The one body function we can control consciously by choice is breathing. Everything else is under automatic, unconscious control. The mind is constantly monitoring the body to maintain homeostasis. If the mind notices a hyperalert state it will continue producing adrenaline or cortisol to cope with the emergency. If we consciously choose to take slow, deep breaths, the monitoring mind is fooled into thinking the emergency is over. It instructs the body to stop producing adrenaline and cortisol and start producing calming chemicals like oxytocin and endorphins. You can easily find many powerful breathing techniques. The simplest often used is box breathing, where we count to four on the in-breath, hold for four, release for four, then hold for four before repeating. From something like 60 breaths a minute, we drop to four.

Take a Break

Another obvious and simple technique for coping when emotions are high is to take a break. It only happens when we first choose to STOP AND THINK. Even a gap of two or three seconds gives space for the green brain to catch up with the red brain, although, of course, longer breaks are more effective. Simple breathing techniques help make the most of a break to calm down. A longer more structured time-out process, as described in Chapter 8, can stop tension from boiling over.

The Anger Volcano

One emotion can trigger another, so we form networks of connected emotions. Loneliness might lead to sadness, which leads to frustration leading to anger. This is sometimes depicted as a volcano where the lava under the ground depicts various emotions bubbling and boiling away. As emotions move nearer the surface, it is like lava being constricted and erupting with great force into the air. Anger has turned to violence. Under our anger may be disappointment, rejection, worthlessness, despair, loneliness, resentment, grief, shame, and much more. Working on those emotions may indicate the underlying cause of our distress and help bring our anger down. Anger can even be triggered by something as simple as hunger or tiredness. This diagram is sometimes depicted as an iceberg with anger above the surface as the visible face of our emotions to others, while all the other emotions lurk below.

Anger is often viewed as a negative emotion; however, anger naturally arises when something happens in our world that does not feel right, typically when we lack a sense of control. Like all emotions, anger can be managed in helpful or unhelpful ways. Anger can give us courage to stand up when things happen that are just not right. The French word for heart is *coeur*, so we can see courage as the rage of the heart. Used wisely and carefully, anger can be constructive and helpful, but when used unwisely results in abuse and violence.

Some people with brain damage are not able to feel or recognise anger. They no longer feel the message their body is telling them that something is not right. They or someone else is doing something that should not be, but without that message, their lives become utterly chaotic. You might like to look up the story of Phineas Gage. We need anger, but we also need to control how we express anger, so it supports resolving difference rather than creating unnecessary conflict.

Distraction

If we take our mind off the emotion and the situation that is causing distress, even for a short while, we allow the green brain time to kick back in, so the person can drop down on the 1–10 scale to a point where they can think more clearly about what is needed in the moment.

There are positive distractions all around us. Any hobby or interest that will engage our interest pulls our mind away from the situation. Soothing activities are ideal. Meditation or relaxation techniques are effective. Suitable music can be powerful. Active exercise also helps reduce adrenaline production.

Be careful not to use a distraction that heightens emotion again, such as violent computer games, heavy music, or alcohol and drugs. Make sure that what you do or where you go is safe.

Mindfulness Skills

Mindfulness has three aspects. The first is awareness of our internal world. The more we are aware of our internal responses, the more we can appreciate the messages our body sends and become more aware of our body's needs. Our internal world includes our emotions and thinking. While our emotions and thinking operate unconsciously, we will create unintended consequences.

The second is to be aware of the external world. We will notice other people's emotions and actions and changes in the world about us. This builds empathy. The third aspect is when we combine our awareness of our inside and the outside and how they are connected.

The more mindful we are, the more we notice clues that a situation might become problematic. Imagine you walk into a bar and notice someone over in the corner becoming louder. If you are alert, you will see the signs that this could turn into a difficult situation and leave.

If you are not as mindful, you sit down with a drink. The person gets louder and harder to ignore. If you still do not notice, an argument may well follow. At this point it is hard to find a way out of the situation and the options available are much reduced. The sooner you become aware of what is happening, the easier it is to cope.

A simple Google search will bring up a treasure trove of mindfulness exercises that build our ability to be aware of our internal environment and external situation. There are many therapies and techniques we use to heal emotions. Some are merely observing in silence and stillness, while others use movement. Some encourage you to keep a particular thought or word in mind, while others try to move away from thinking. All are valuable but you will find what works for you.

The commercialisation of mindfulness in recent years has seen it used as a way of blocking out negative experiences. It should not be used to push ourselves into putting up with harmful practices or ignoring negativity. Thich Nhat Hanh[1] taught Engaged Buddhism, in which mindfulness is used to be aware of the world around us and encourages action to make a better world. He states that it is through our full engagement with the violence in the world and ourselves, that we find a pathway to break the cycle of pain and suffering.

Distress Tolerance

If a problem arises that we can solve, we should solve it. Often, however, we cannot or choose not to solve the problem. When that happens, we must cope with the anxiety that arises because of the problem. We each have a certain capacity to cope with stress and distress. It is like a bucket with water being poured into it. We can contain a certain level of anxiety, but there comes a point where we are no longer able to contain it. Our distress tolerance is insufficient to cope and our bucket overflows. We feel overwhelmed and often return to previous unconscious habit patterns or other ineffective ways of coping, which make the situation even worse. We can learn to improve our coping skills to contain greater levels of distress. Some of us can not only contain our own levels of stress but can also contain other people's anxiety. High-powered politicians or those in the helping professions contain high levels of stress for others. People will use an addiction that reduces the immediate feeling of anxiety, but in fact, just recycles water back in the top of the bucket again.

In Dunedin, New Zealand in 1973 an experiment began in which the parents of 1000 newborn babies were approached and asked to bring their children in every two years for a wide range of tests and measurements on all aspects of their lives.[2] Those children are now in their fifties, so an enormous database of detailed information has been gathered about them. The researchers analysed all the data collected over the years seeking links between the children's early life and their later life outcomes.

One analysis of the data identified the most successful people of the 1000 and investigated what they had in common when they were young. We might think the determining factors would be parents' income or the school they attended, but the quality that stood out as the single most important characteristic was distress tolerance.

When schoolwork becomes boring, a child with distress tolerance skills will not give up. They will cope with other children's annoying behaviours and tensions between themselves and teachers. They will tend to do better at school, have more friends, get better jobs, and earn more money later in life.

They will get on better with authorities and keep on at sports or projects when others would give up. They will stick to their fitness programme at the gym. Good distress tolerance skills allow a child to get on better with other people and have friends to call on when times get tough. They will not get swayed by unhealthy food and will save for their future. When you consider all of this, it becomes apparent why distress tolerance is such an important learnable skill.

The levels of distress tolerance in three-year-olds were measured in the Dunedin study by the Marshmallow test devised at Stanford University. A researcher enters a room with a marshmallow on a plate. The child is told that the researcher has some more marshmallows in the office that they will go and find. If the original marshmallow is still there on their return 15 minutes later, they receive a second marshmallow. You can watch videos on the internet of children taking the marshmallow test. Some eat the marshmallow straight away. Others gaze intently until they are unable to resist anymore. Others hold on. Even at their age, they have developed the skill of using a distraction. They will play with a toy, sing a song, draw a picture, or hide under that table. What better skill can you teach a child to prepare them for life as an adult? Simple techniques like waiting for a reward can teach this skill.

Emotions are a part of the red brain. If we do not have sufficient control over our emotions, we will remain stuck in the present moment. Once we have a level of control over emotions, we can use techniques to gain control over our thinking.

Thinking Well-being

Emotions tell us how we feel in the moment, but that is not sufficient to make a good decision. We need to engage our thinking, particularly to ensure that we consider the future implications of our proposed actions and that we engage our empathy to consider the impact of our actions on others. There are well-established techniques like CBT, DBT, and ACT, discussed in the next chapter, that work on belief systems and thinking styles. A systems view places such techniques in a wider framework to include the body, and social and spiritual aspects to make them even more powerful. We will start with an overview of a whole human being using a model from the Māori people of New Zealand that fits easily into systems ideas and provides a foundation for exploring the three main approaches above.

Te Whare Tapa Whā

Sir Mason Durie of the Rangitāne, Ngāti Kauwhata, and Ngāti Raukawa tribes developed a Māori model of health that holds deeper truths within a deceptively simple metaphor. Te Whare Tapa Whā is a reference to the four walls of the house. Just as a house has four walls, a human being has four interconnected aspects. They are body (tinana), social and relationships (whānau), mind (hinengaro), and spirit (wairua).

There is no house without walls and there are no walls without a house. No wall stands independently, so each of the four aspects is bound together and supports the others for the building to stand. A person needs a strong and balanced body, mind, social/relationships, and spirit.

The house must be built on the land (Papatūānuku) and under the sky (Ranginui). It is embedded in the environment, just as we are. The house is traditionally understood to be a particular tribal ancestor, so entering the house is to journey into the embodied ancestor. Large wooden carvings (Poupou) stand around the walls depicting the tribal ancestors and their histories. We walk into the past. We carry our past with us in all we do. We carry both the wonderful cultural heritage and history that has cumulatively been built over the generations, and the trauma, tragedy, and sins of past generations that they were unable to resolve.

My grandfather fought in World War I at Gallipoli and later worked in military hospitals in England witnessing horrific scenes that haunted him for the rest of his life. His experiences impacted his ability to be a parent, traumatising his two children, my mother, and uncle, which ultimately had a significant impact on who I am today, even though I have no personal memory of him.

Māori place great emphasis on knowing about their ancestors and the lives they lived. The trauma from the past we can resolve by bringing it into consciousness ends with us. What we cannot resolve is passed on to future generations.

An interesting gathering (hui) was held in 1986, between the Ngāpuhi tribes of the far north of New Zealand and tribes from the Bay of Plenty further south. When the Mātaatua canoe first landed in New Zealand some 600 or more years ago, a disagreement arose as to whether the canoe was given to Ngāpuhi to move north or whether they stole it. The hui reconciled their differences and reaffirmed their shared genealogical links, healing a centuries-old wound, and freeing future generations from an unconscious cultural wound.

A Māori proverb says, "Kia whakatōmuri te haere whakamua", which means, "We walk backwards into the future. with my eyes fixed on the past". It means that we need to be aware of our past and how it has made us what we are before we can move successfully into the future. We use our experience of the past to make sense of the present moment and form plausible projections of likely futures to guide our decisions in the present.

The tekoteko on top of the house at the front commonly depicts a warrior with a weapon of some type in their hands. They are on guard for any threats to the people. We could see this as our awareness, reflecting our need to remain alert to what is happening in our world.

The area of land in front of the wharenui is called marae ātea, where formal speech-making usually occurs when visitors arrive. It is said to belong to the realm of Tūmatauenga, the god of war. It is the arena where conflict is resolved, so peace may prevail inside the wharenui. The pōwhiri is an elaborate traditional welcoming ritual allowing host and visitor to realise their connectedness by taking away the tapu (sacredness, restrictions), and other differences that divide them. The manuhiri (visitors) then become noa (ordinary). Figure 5.1 shows the various parts of a wharenui.

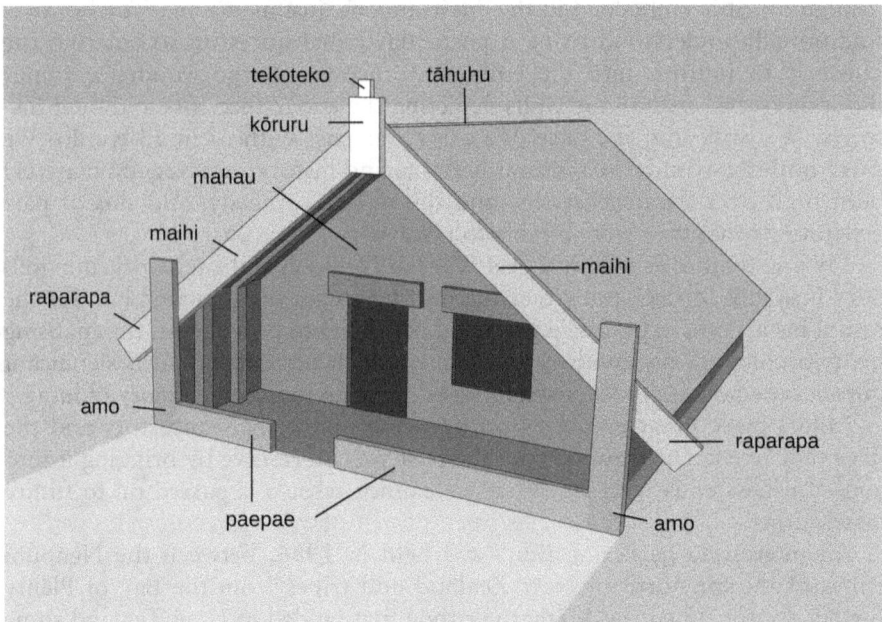

Figure 5.1 Named parts of a traditional Māori Meetinghouse.   Maihi, Wharenui outer parts, https://commons.wikimedia.org/wiki/File:Maihi.jpg, Rudolph89, Creative Commons Attribution-Share Alike 4.0 International license.

The Four Walls

Each wall can be analysed through the *Dynamics of Life* model. Each has primary systems and shadow systems. Each processes energy, matter, and information to do work and has entropy that cannot be contained. Sometimes that entropy is passed between the walls.

The first wall is the physical or tinana. It is those things we can touch and feel in the world. We use our body to interact with the world. We can do this in ways that enhance or detract from our well-being. Exercise, diet, sleep and rest, warmth, hygiene, and sometimes medications all build tinana. Adequate housing, money, and transport are needed to live in the physical world. Addictions and unhealthy living detract from a healthy tinana.

The second wall is the mind or hinengaro. This is not visible, but it is very real. From an enactive viewpoint, emotions and thinking arise from the body and introduce a greater complexity that enables added flexibility.

The place of intuition also fits in the mind. Intuition might arise as a whole new level of cognition, or it might be the self-organising of all the existing aspects (body, emotion, and thinking, and social). There is also a gut intuition that is more related to body wisdom. Our values and beliefs arose from how we were raised and from past experiences. Our beliefs and values drive our thinking and emotions. Beliefs and values are shaped by culture and worldview.

The third wall is the social wall called whānau, which is usually translated as family. For Māori, whānau includes members of the extended family spanning generations, as well as cousins and second cousins. From a Māori point of view, whānau is not just an important part of life, it is who I am. I am my whānau. They say "Ehara taku toa i te toa takitahi, engari he toa takitini", meaning my strength does not come from me alone, but rather from my connectedness to others.

There is a strong focus on genealogy (Whakapapa) in Māori, so whānau also extends into the past. Like boundaries that reveal and conceal, genealogy both links and divides. People feel connected when there is a common ancestor, but it can divide when people are told they do not belong, or their lineage is from an inferior line.

We have many social relationships. They include work, sport, recreation, cultural and spiritual relationships, and friendships. Social relationships will only flourish if we put energy into building them and allow trust to grow. Relationships are all about resolving difference between ourselves and others.

The final wall is the spiritual. In Māori, this is wairua. Wai means water and rua means two. Our physical body is around 70% water. Wairua is the second spiritual water that flows through our being. Spirituality means very different things to different people. It is the place where we feel whole and connected to who we really are, as well as being connected to others, and to the world we live in. It is the place we go to find ourselves and find a sense of peace amid the chaos of everyday life.

For some, spirituality means attending a church or temple and following a set of beliefs. For others, it is climbing a mountain or going to the seaside. For yet others, it is music, art, meditation, or prayer. There is a strong connection between spirituality and culture.

We all have such a place, although some people may not have found it. Beyond the hurly-burly of daily life, it is a refuge where we ponder questions like, "What is my life all about?", "Why am I here?" and "What happens when I die?"

The overlaps and interconnections between the walls are clear. Any one element in any wall will have an impact on the whole house. As an example, if my sleep and rest are inadequate, it will impact my emotions and thinking. This impacts on my relationships with those around me and detracts from my spiritual well-being. If I start an exercise programme, my health will improve, lifting all the other walls.

You may have noticed the resonance between Te Whare Tapa Whā, and Gregg Henriques' Tree of Knowledge. Tinana relates to the life level, hinengaro to the mind, whānau to the social, and the spiritual becomes the highest level.

Having found a holistic overview of a human being from Māori culture which is in harmony with systems ideas, we can progress to explore tools that can be used to make ourselves more effective at different levels of functioning. As we learned from Te Whare Tapa Whā, a tool used well from one wall often impacts positively on other walls.

Key Points

1 There are three approaches to changing behaviour: emotional regulation, awareness, and reframing beliefs and values.
2 Emotional tolls include the 1:10 scale, distraction, taking a break, and the anger volcano.
3 Building awareness is self-awareness, awareness of the outside world, and an awareness of the connection between the two.
4 Developing distress tolerance skills.
5 Te Whare Tapa Whā recognised four aspects of a human being: body (tinana), mind (hinengaro), family/relationships (whānau), and spirit (wairua). The strategies, tools, and techniques explained in this chapter are simple ideas, but they only work if they are put into practice.

Notes

1 See *Interbeing: Fourteen Guidelines for Engaged Buddhism* by Thich Nhat Hanh.
2 https://dunedinstudy.otago.ac.nz/.

Bibliography

Durie, M. (1998). *Whaiora: Maori Health Development* (2nd edition). Oxford University Press. https://www.amazon.com/Whaiora-Maori-Health-Development-1998-10-01/dp/B01FGPAFWG/ref=monarch_sidesheet

Hanh, T. N. (1987). *Interbeing: Fourteen Guidelines for Engaged Buddhism*. Parallax Press. http://www.amazon.com/Interbeing-Fourteen-Guidelines-Engaged-Buddhism/dp/1888375086

Hanh, T. N. (1995). *Peace is Every Step*. Rider: An imprint of Ebury Publishing.

Kabat-Zinn, J. (2009). *Wherever You Go, There You Are: Mindfulness Meditation in Everyday Life: A Guide to your Place in the Universe and an Inquiry into Who and What You Are*. Piatkus.

Chapter 6

Extended Cognitive Behaviour Theory

Introduction

Cognitive Behaviour Therapy (CBT) is an effective practice widely used to address unhealthy belief systems that lead people to poor decision-making.[1] From a systems perspective, combining it with Te Whare Tapa Whā makes it even more effective, as demonstrated in Figure 6.1. Cognitive Behaviour Theory, as it was taught to me, proposes a linear chain in which we have core beliefs that shape how we interpret any event. We then think about the event, which sets off an emotion, leading to a decision, and action that creates an outcome.

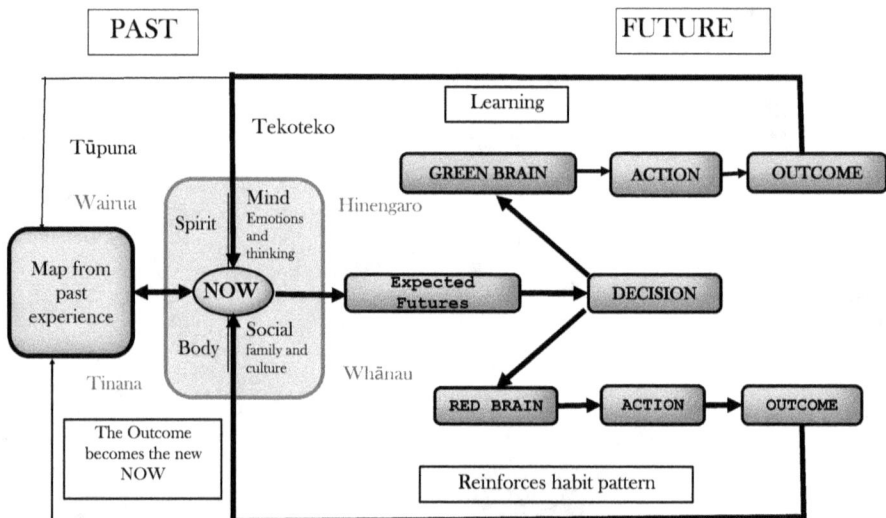

Figure 6.1 We experience any event through our whole being. Then we decide whether to use the red brain or the green brain to generate an outcome which becomes the new event.

DOI: 10.4324/9781003533641-6

Core beliefs – Event – Thought – Emotion – Decision – Action – Outcome

We can choose an automatic habit-based (red brain) thought, or a deliberate alternative (green brain) thought, leading to different outcomes.

CBT has successfully helped people gain control over violence, smoking cessation, anxiety, addiction, etc. but it does not integrate the body into its framework and has a very Western focus on the individual. This is in stark contrast with the African concept of, ubuntu, which states that "I am because we are".

We experience ourselves and our world through our whole being, not simply the thinking and emotions proposed in CBT. Rather, we experience through our body, mind, relationships, and spirit, recursively, all at the same time. Our experience is interpreted through our values and beliefs which are distilled from past experiences. We mindfully appreciate our internal and external experiences to project likely future outcomes to act and create an end result.

Cognitive Behaviour Therapy (CBT), Acceptance and Commitment Therapy (ACT), and Dialectic Behaviour Therapy (DBT)

Arising out of CBT is the process of Acceptance and Commitment Therapy (ACT), developed by Stephen Hayes. In this tradition the acceptance part of ACT is concerned with coping with and accepting uncomfortable emotions through the use of mindfulness techniques. This builds the strength to avoid becoming reactive in situations, which often only makes them worse than they need to be. Having mastered this approach, we can reframe thinking patterns towards a more positive and useful way of responding to problems.

Dialectic Behaviour Therapy (DBT), developed by Marsha Linehan, is another adaptation of CBT, which stresses the importance of emotional regulation and distress tolerance using mindfulness techniques. DBT particularly acknowledges the importance of the body in both identifying and regulating emotions. Both DBT and ACT recognise that suffering arises out of the avoidance of uncomfortable emotions which impact our ability to think and plan. DBT is more educational, while ACT is more experiential in nature, but neither includes either social or spiritual aspects.

Gregg Henriques states that if we know where a blockage is located in someone's psyche, we can find an appropriate technique to resolve it. Another thinker, Bruce Perry, reminds us that until the emotions can be regulated, attempts to control thinking will prove ineffective.

CBT proposes a linear chain which involves thinking first, whereas a systems perspective suggests that all aspects of our being arise simultaneously. Accordingly, within such an approach all aspects influence and modify all others in recursive, repeating feedback loops. If it is seen in terms of a race, it is more likely that thinking follows after the more immediate body and emotional response.

CBT does grasp the importance of thinking. The final step before acting is usually a thought such as "Right, I think I will buy it". This might not necessarily be put into the form of words. There is, for example, a whole world of sense-making that does not rely on language. This is filled with images, movement, and feeling. After all, even primitive animals are quite capable of complex cognitive processing without using language.

If I follow a preset habitual pattern arising from my red brain, the decision will generally be the same as in the past. Each time I repeat the habit pattern, it is reinforced and becomes stronger. Conversely, if I use my green brain, I rationally assess the overall situation. I seek other perspectives, consider alternative future outcomes, or ask who might be affected. This means rather than a one-size-fits-all red brain solution, I generate a specific green brain solution. I can still make an error, but I am much more likely to make a better decision, especially if the situation is complex. When I choose an alternative thought I can learn from the event. Accordingly, in future, I will have a wider repertoire of responses to cope with any situations that arise.

Gregory Bateson[2] noted levels of learning:

Learning 0 Just repeating the same habitual pattern
Learning 1 Choosing from an existing set of choices
Learning 2 Learning a new response that did not exist before
Learning 3 Learning how to learn.

Whether I choose a red or a green brain approach, the outcome becomes the next event, thereby forming a feedback loop. That means we are constantly sensing, making-sense, and responding to the situations in our lives. Thinking back to Robert Rosen's work on anticipation, the feedback loop includes projecting likely future outcomes before making a decision. This highlights the importance of stopping to adequately think about the problem at hand. We should consider all relevant options in order to gain a wider perspective.

When thinking, we tend to focus on the implications of the decision we make. We do not notice the implications of the options not chosen, although these may be significant. If I buy new clothes, for example, I might put off repaying a debt to a friend.

Values and Beliefs Cards

Beliefs and values are a core part of CBT. Our beliefs and values are embedded in our cognitive mapping. We act according to our beliefs and values, which directly impact the outcomes in our lives. Clarifying and refining values is helpful. The values card exercise is better done with someone to guide the process and ask questions. A full list of the *values cards* is given in the Appendix and can be downloaded from victormacgill.com. Many of the cards are vague in nature and might be true in some situations but not others. This invites discussion. There are no right or wrong cards, but beliefs have consequences, so it is good to ask whether your beliefs and values take you closer or further from your dreams. Any value we espouse gives us "permission" to do what the value says. If I believe, for instance, that "It's OK to hit someone if they deserve it", then I permit myself to use violence.

Take the cards one at a time and place them on the floor in one of four groups, but not on top of each other so they all remain visible. One group is to be for values you believe are true. The second group is for values the person used to hold but which they have now abandoned. The third group is for cards they do not currently believe, but which they would like to hold. Some people find they cannot trust others, but feel that they perhaps might in the future. The final cluster is for all those other values which they have never believed in.

Once the exercise is completed, start with the final group of cards of things: those beliefs never yet held. Typically, this pile is filled with negative or harmful beliefs; sometimes, however, there are values worth reconsidering such as cards with a religious overtone or those addressing notions of trusting people.

Next, turn to the second group of cards: those values previously believed in or perhaps which might have been often heard while growing up, and which might still have made an impact. These cards demonstrate our ability to change our minds. We have all done it before. It is good to reaffirm a person's ability to change their beliefs and talk about how they did it and why it had been positive to let go of a belief once held.

Next, look to the third group; beliefs they would like to be able to believe. This can give an indication of future beliefs they might embrace. Finally, come to the group of values they do believe. People can generally divide these cards into three or four themes, such as "Family comes first", "Look after your mates", or "Life is hard". Sometimes one of the cards represents the whole group, or you may find new words might be sought to describe each group.

You are left with a small number of key concepts that provide a concise overview of the person's worldview. Remember that these values tend to be the conscious values and might better reflect their ideals rather than lived reality. Ask the person how well these categories fit with how they see the world and how well they work for them. Themes may contradict each other or need to be balanced. If any themes stand out as being unhelpful, discuss what alternative values would be useful. You can discuss whether those values are being consistently lived and explore the implications of their beliefs for other people.

Horse and Coach Model

The Horse and Coach Model is a useful metaphor, devised by the author, to understand the various parts of a person and how they interact, as depicted in Figure 6.2. The whole "horse and coach" represents a person. The horses and coach will only reach their destination if all the parts work together effectively.

The horses are like our emotions. They are powerful and provide the energy to move the coach to the destination. Without the horses, the coach cannot move. Our emotions also move us powerfully towards our goals. It is very interesting that the word emotion has the term "motion" in it, and emotion gives us *motivation*. When we feel a strong emotion, we talk of being *moved*.

If horses are allowed to go where they want, the result will be chaos. Horses can get spooked and bolt; in the same way, an inappropriate fight/flight response results in reactive behaviours. You may know people led by their emotions without stopping to consider their actions. They end up in places they did not want or expect.

A skilful driver needs to tie the horses together in order to harness their energy. The driver is our thinking and sense-making, who skilfully cares for the horses, feeding, watering, and resting them. The horses still get to run, which they love, but now the running is channelled so the whole horse and coach gains the benefit.

At times, the driver will speed the horses up, slow them down, or turn left or right as necessary. We use our thinking to control our emotions and ensure they do not get out of hand.

The driver undertakes other critical roles. They must remain alert and aware, watching the road ahead and noticing any hazards such as landslides, heavy rain, or changes to the road. We need to anticipate future obstacles before they arise and formulate a plan to cope. The driver has a map from the passenger to guide the journey, just as we have a cognitive map that guides our lives. The more accurate and up to date the map, the more likely they will reach the destination in time. The driver should take advantage of opportunities to talk to other drivers and people encountered along the journey,

Figure 6.2 The Horse and Coach Model. The horses are our emotions, thinking is the driver, the coach is the body, and the passenger is our beliefs and values.   Shutterstock, Kitichan, https://www.shutterstock.com/image-vector/legend-wild-western-american-four-wheeled-2250613831, passenger deleted.

sharing information and knowledge that will help make sure the coach runs effectively. It is important to share ideas and collaborate for everyone's benefit. On the road, there will be other coaches. There are road rules to be obeyed and courtesies that will ensure everybody's safe passage just as we use our social skills in daily life.

An addiction is like a shortcut that appears to be an easier road. However, as soon as the horse and coach travel around the bend, the road becomes bumpier and more difficult. The addiction road leads to the same familiar place, which is far away from the intended destination. A clever driver is not tempted by an unhelpful shortcut.

Next, the driver must maintain the coach. Parts become worn and need to be replaced, cleaned, and repaired. The coach is our body, so we use our thinking to maintain our health and well-being. The driver is firmly connected to the coach, and the horses are firmly tied to the coach, just as the body, emotions, and thinking are all linked together. There is baggage on top of the coach. We carry "emotional baggage", collected through our past actions, that interferes with our ability to cope with the situations in which we find ourselves. If the luggage is too heavy, or not tied down properly, it might fall off. Someone could get hurt, or your luggage might spill open for everyone to see.

The driver needs to be alert for anything that might impact the journey. It is like our sense of awareness. If we are not aware of our bodily sensations, our emotional state, or the nature of our thoughts, we will never learn better ways of responding to the challenges posed by life.

The final part is the passenger, who travels in the coach. The passenger represents our values and beliefs. Our values and beliefs arise from our interpretations of our past experiences. Just as the driver looks to the front, the passenger looks back at the scenery already passed. We use our interpretations and awareness of the patterns of the past to map likely future outcomes.

The passenger chooses the destination. The thoughts and feelings that arise out of our past experiences determine where we choose to go in our lives. The passenger gives the driver the map because our cognitive mapping defines our beliefs and values. If the passenger wants to go to Blenheim from Nelson in New Zealand, for example a lazy driver will merely load up and head off. This represents the situation in which an old habit pattern is repeated with the same results as before. The aware driver will anticipate upcoming hazards and discuss them with the passenger. They may choose a different destination, take a different route, or delay the travel to create a more fulfilling and productive trip.

We need to continually reflect on our values and beliefs, reassessing them so they take us where we want in our lives. There is a direct link between our values and beliefs, and our thoughts and emotions. Our thoughts, emotions, and body reactions arise out of our interpretation of the events we experience. Two people in the same situation will have different interpretations and thus different experiences.

All parts of the horse and coach are needed, but the driver has to play many crucial roles. As with all models, this is a gross simplification of what really happens. All the processes are intertwined and depend upon each other. The captain of a ship may make the most crucial decisions for running the ship, but this is only a small portion of all the decisions made to ensure the whole ship runs smoothly. Decisions are made at all levels appropriate to the needs and characteristics of that level.

Blame, Deny, Justify, and Minimise

We generally accept and integrate experiences we find pleasing and positive. We would rather exclude other experiences, which trigger shame, guilt, embarrassment, resentment, anger, fear, sadness, and other uncomfortable emotions. There might be a punishment to avoid, a reward we will miss, or we might face social rejection. The event might be so traumatic that we become overwhelmed and must shut down to avoid disintegration.

When we deflect what we are unwilling or unable to embrace as a part of life, we pass on the 'hot potato' of emotional energy for someone else to manage. A racist person will react in a social situation in a way that is likely to trigger others. The racist may not like other people's responses to their actions. Until we learn to accept the unacceptable, the feedback loop will continue to recreate the same future until we change.

We deflect those events using four main techniques. The first is to deny that the event ever happened. We simply blot out the event entirely, or tell someone a direct lie. A person might deny involvement in a situation: deny speeding, deny having said something, deny violence, deny a debt, or whatever.

The second method of avoiding is minimising. When we deny, we shut off the whole event, but when we minimise, we accept and acknowledge some of it and reject the rest. We make it smaller. We might, for example, deny driving at 120 km/h, but acknowledge that we were driving at 110 km/h. We might acknowledge certain words spoken but deny others. A push might be acknowledged when it was actually a punch.

The third method is blaming. As with all these avoidance strategies, we all blame at some point. We acknowledge the event but deny responsibility. Somebody or something else is scapegoated and held responsible. The other person started the argument, someone else forgot, the government is out to get me, my brakes failed.

Finally, we justify the event. We create a story that is not true, but is nevertheless persuasive enough to sound plausible; "I just got so busy I couldn't come", "I did not know it would go so late", "I could not say no", and so forth.

You will notice that we can have a mix of these various methods. I might deny or minimise being responsible for an event by blaming someone else and creating a story to justify why I am not responsible.

But we are trying to avoid an event we have already experienced. It is already a part of us. Whenever we are unwilling or unable to accept an experience consciously, the emotions that were linked to the event descend and constellate in our unconscious mind. Here we hold all our resentment, disappointment, guilt and shame, embarrassment, rejection, fear, anger, sadness, and more. We are stuck with the hot potato.

We can see this in terms of our *Dynamics of Life* model. We experience events. Those situations we can process and integrate become a part of our primary self. Those parts we cannot integrate are denied, minimised, blamed on others, or justified. As they are expelled into the outside world, they descend into our shadow system. Our actions resisting the world loop back. Lessons we have not learned keep returning until we respond in an adequate manner.

Our suppressed emotions become like a sack carried on our backs everywhere we go which only weighs us down and makes our journey more difficult. Carl Jung calls this our *shadow* because it is dark and foreboding and our shadow remains with us everywhere we go. You can see this represented in Figure 6.3.

Whenever we experience a similar event to the initial suppressed event, the old emotion may rise again, usually in unhelpful ways. A person bitten by a dog when young might develop a fear of dogs. Many years later, when they come across a small, docile dog a feeling of dread and fear still arises. A dog faced with a person showing dread and fear for no apparent reason is likely

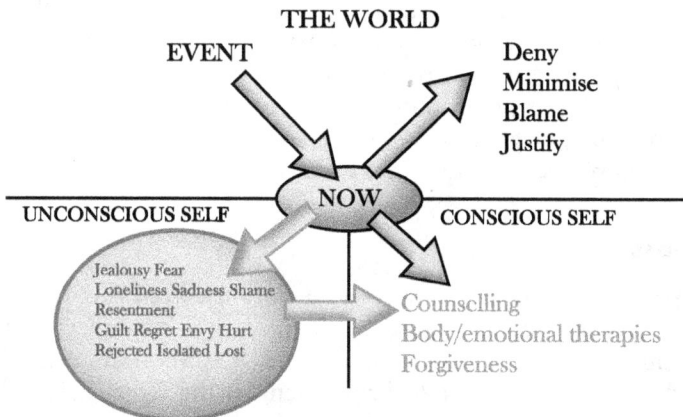

Figure 6.3 When we reject an event by denying, minimising, blaming, or justifying, the emotion becomes suppressed and must be brought to light in order for us to heal.

to react defensively and growl. The person becomes even more afraid. Especially when two people trigger each other, the situation can ratchet up and escalate quickly.

Carl Jung interestingly also writes about the "golden shadow". There are aspects of our nature that are so wonderful and amazing that we become afraid of them and find ourselves unable to integrate them. The responsibility of living up to our full potential can be so terrifying and overwhelming that those magnificent aspects of ourselves are also suppressed and enter the recessive shadow.

Yet another perspective is to see this through a mythological lens. As we grow, we all create a shadow that appears in fairy stories as a dragon, a monster, an evil witch, or a wizard. For example, Sleeping Beauty's father wanted to shelter his daughter from the pain and suffering of life. This was a vain hope. Sooner or later, we must confront reality. Similarly, the Buddha's father tried to hide suffering and death from his son. Life in a castle is a metaphor for this existence; any attempt to create a boundary that shuts out pain and suffering, but it is doomed to fail. There will always be a time for the prince or princess to leave the castle and as soon as that happens the dragon, the shadow, or the suppressed emotion, stirs within its lair and rises up. It must be overcome. When the dragon is defeated, there is a wedding, or a treasure is found.

As emotions are suppressed, they move into our muscles and affect our posture and body movement. Our body takes on the shape of the demon of the emotions we are unable to adequately express until we find a way to release them.

So, how do we "kill the dragon" and retrieve the treasure? We bring the unconscious emotions out from the unconscious into the conscious world. There is an uncomfortable boundary to be crossed. To heal, the emotion must re-enter the present moment. It is usually so uncomfortable and painful that we leave it where it is. If there is a safe enough atmosphere – perhaps through counselling or other talking therapies, bodywork releasing trapped energy on the body, or perhaps meditation – healing occurs. A powerful tool for bringing suppressed emotion into consciousness is forgiveness.

Forgiveness

One key strategy to healing suppressed emotions and bringing them back into conscious awareness is forgiveness. Some people misunderstand forgiveness as letting someone off the hook. Rather, it is an attempt to choose to release suppressed emotions and bring them to the light. It is an internal process of healing, which is independent of the other person. It may be useful to gain forgiveness from the wronged person, but it is not essential. This means we can still forgive people who have left our lives.

Forgiveness acknowledges that what happened was bad and wrong and should not have happened. It acknowledges the hurt and suffering caused.

The emotions that arose because of those experiences have become trapped inside, hindering our ability to act in the present. By releasing the emotion, we are no longer triggered when similar events recur, leaving us in a better place to act effectively. The other person is still responsible for their actions and must face the consequences they created.

I have developed my own forgiveness process, adapting the writings of Dr Guy Pettit, whose workshop manual is free and accessible through the internet[3] and goes into much greater depth than is discussed here. I work with a person on a whiteboard, but it could be written on a piece of paper. It is better to work with another person rather than by yourself, because they can offer you support as old emotions rise to the surface.

The process starts with the person they wish to forgive. Five columns are drawn, as in Table 6.1. In the first column list the person's positive aspects, what attracted them to the person being forgiven, and how they have helped enrich their life. In the next column write all the ways that person being

Table 6.1 The forgiveness process

What were the wonderful gifts, experiences and qualities of the other person that enriched your life?	What are the ways in which the other person harmed or hurt you?	What do you know about the person that helps you understand why events turned out as they did, especially thinking of their earlier experiences?	What emotions arose in you as a result of having been hurt?	
What were the wonderful gifts and experiences, and qualities that you gave to the other person that enriched their life?	What are the ways in which you have harmed or hurt the other person?	What do you know about yourself that helps you explain your actions?	What are the emotions you feel now as you realise and feel the ways you have hurt the other person? What emotions might the person have felt because of your actions?	What future would you prefer now that you have been able to release those emotions that have held you back?

forgiven has harmed or wounded them, or caused them pain and distress. The third column asks what you know about the person being forgiven which might help explain why they acted as they did. It is helpful to reflect on the trauma in their life and its impact on them. The fourth column lists the emotions that arise for the person forgiving as they confront the ways they have been hurt. You may well find there are techniques such as breathing techniques or bodywork that help you to connect with those emotions.

As the emotions arise let them flow, ensuring a safe environment for everybody present. Work through the questions on the top row and formulate a forgiveness sentence to go in the fifth column, which might read something like:

> William abandoned me when I really needed help, I was hurt and felt loss, rejection, and confusion. I now release those emotions I have held onto for so long, freeing me to live a full, vibrant life.

Once written, get the person forgiving to stand or get in a comfortable position. Focus on calm breathing and build body awareness. Read through the list of emotions or have someone else read the emotions again and, though it may be uncomfortable, feel the emotion and make it as real as possible. Then read the sentence out loud three times, getting louder each time. People can find this very helpful, but it can be intense, and the person may need support and encouragement.

The next step is to repeat the process about the person who is forgiving in relation to the person they are forgiving in row 2. In the first column of this part of the table write the good things they contributed to the relationship with the person being forgiven. In the second column write the person's thoughts or actions, intended or otherwise, that caused harm or hurt. They confront themselves and recognise how their actions have fallen short of what could have been. What emotions probably arose for the person being forgiven? What are the emotions that arise for the forgiver in this moment as they confront your own actions? They can then write a sentence forgiving themselves for their actions and the impact of those actions.

When that process is complete, if appropriate, the person may wish to write about how you would like your relationship with that person to be in the future and what you would have to do to bring that future about. Now that constricting emotions have been released, you are in a much stronger position to act more fully and effectively and not to be constrained by sabotaging reactions. The process can be repeated for other people or other events in your life. It may even be of value to repeat a forgiveness process already completed. Dr Guy Pettit, for example, uses muscle testing to test whether a process is complete, or if there is more to be released. I attended a full weekend workshop with him where there was plenty of time for emotions to arise and be dealt with. In my work, by contrast, I must squeeze everything into a one-hour session. Most people are fine following the session, but there is a risk that I release emotions without the time to support that person afterwards. Accordingly, I deliberately tone down the process to make it manageable. Ideally, there should be time to support the person doing the forgiving. I alert people to the fact that emotions may arise after they leave and that they should recognise and release emotions should they arise.

Key Points

1 Cognitive Behaviour Therapy (CBT) has helped many people, but it is limited by its linear structure and its lack of body connection
2 CBT and Te Whare Tapa Whā can be integrated to form a much more effective and practical tool for changing behaviour
3 Values cards are a useful tool for exploring belief systems
4 The Horse and Coach Model is an easy metaphor to describe the parts of a human being and how they interact
5 Events we are unable to integrate into our being do not go away; rather, the emotion sinks into the unconscious
6 Forgiveness is a powerful tool to release suppressed emotion from previous trauma.

Notes

1 See *Cognitive Behaviour Therapy: Basics and Beyond* by Aaron Beck.
2 See https://openresearch.surrey.ac.uk/esploro/outputs/conferencePresentation/ Batesons-Levels-Of-Learning-a-Framework/99516257702346#file-0.
3 http://ww1.iloveulove.org/ (Now only available through The Wayback Machine), https://aap-psychosynthesis.org/resources/Pictures/Articles/forgivenessandhealth. pdf.

Bibliography

Beck, A. T. (1979). *Cognitive Therapy and the Emotional Disorders*. Penguin Publishing Group. https://books.google.com/books?hl=en&lr=&id=nSFvAAAAQ BAJ&pgis=1
Beck, J. S. (2021). *Cognitive Behavior Therapy: Basics and Beyond*. Guilford Press.
Hayes, S., Stroshal, K., & Wilson, K. (2016). *Acceptance and Commitment Therapy: The Process and Practice of Mindful Change* (2nd Edition, Ed.). Gilford Press. https://www.bookdepository.com/Acceptance-and-Commitment-Therapy-Steven-C.-Hayes/9781462528943?redirected=true&utm_medium=Google&utm_campaign=Base1&utm_source=NZ&utm_content=Acceptance-and-Commitment-Therapy&selectCurrency=NZD&w=AF7CAU96124BZ3A8VT46&gclid
Linehan, M. (1987). Dialectical Behavior Therapy for Borderline Personality Disorder: Theory and Method. *Bulletin of the Menninger Clinic*, 51(3), 261–276. https://search. proquest.com/openview/8dcf9549f2165cdeca6d6644cbba7bb2/1?pq-origsite= gscholar&cbl=1818298

Linehan, M. M., & Dimeff, L. (2001). Dialectic Behaviour Theory in a Nutshell. *The California Psychologist*, 34, 10–13. https://doi.org/10.1016/0022-3999(97)90059-3

Tosey, P. (2006). Bateson's Levels of Learning: A Framework for Transformative Learning. *Universities' Forum for Human Resource Development Conference.* http://epubs.surrey.ac.uk/1198/1/fulltext.pdf

Chapter 7

Human Relationships

Introduction

We have explored the *Dynamics of Life* model from basic living systems to the psychological level. At this point the level of complexity leaps yet again to the social level, where human beings interact and communicate with each other. This chapter tends to focus on intimate relationships, which continues in the following chapter and expands to examine whole-family dynamics. We also reveal strategies and techniques for improving social relationships.

When two or more people meet, the dynamics become more complex, as is shown in Figure 7.1. As well as two people meeting, all the subsystems within each of them meet, triggering a wide range of recursive interactions between them, all of which are working to resolve differences. Whatever cannot be resolved, is projected and passed on to the other.

Most intimate relationships are between men and women, but today there is a much greater acknowledgment and acceptance of a range of genders and sexual orientations people choose in intimate relationships with each other.

The Te Whare Tapa Whā model demonstrated the complexities within an individual. We now put two houses together so that each aspect interacts recursively with every aspect of the other. Each one changes the other and is, in turn, changed by the other in real time within a wider environment. Both people assess the likely future actions of the other and pre-empt them by changing their actions, inducing the other to change. As complex as this sounds, we almost always cope flawlessly without even really noticing what we are doing. Imagine, for instance, the complexities of two people walking up a set of stairs, each holding a cup of coffee, discussing world politics, and avoiding people coming the other way.

People's rule sets will always differ. Sometimes the differences are minor and can be accommodated; at other times they divide and separate. Some people are more focused on themselves, while others are more outgoing. Some are open to change, while others resist change.

You attract people and situations that react to your expelled disorder. There is a complementarity between people and the partners they choose.

DOI: 10.4324/9781003533641-7

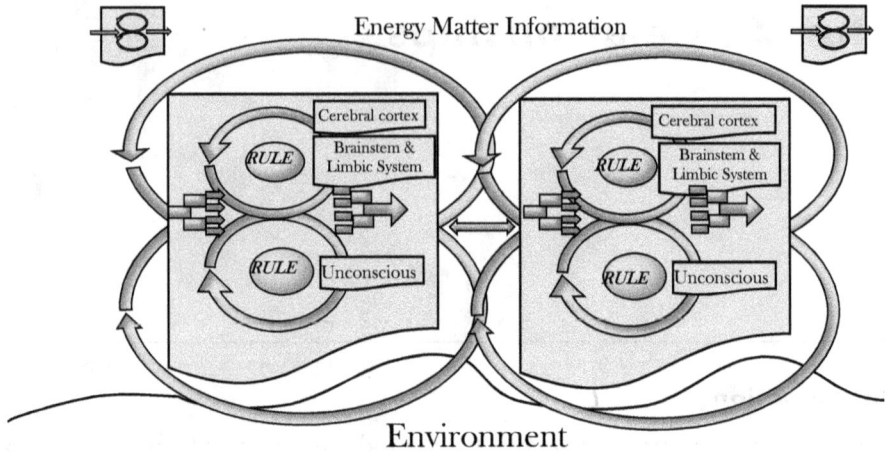

Figure 7.1 Two people interacting in structural coupling.

Partners come together in a mutual dance playing with the unresolved conflict to heal or harm. The witch and the clown[1] is a common archetypal relationship dynamic, in which the man is a clumsy and incompetent clown. This infuriates the woman, who becomes nagging and cold, further impacting the clown's ability to stand confidently. This can devolve into destructive relationship patterns.

A person skilled at resolving entropy tends to attract someone who is also skilful at resolving entropy. Conversely, people not skilled at resolving entropy will attract people living similarly chaotic lives. People who learn from their errors will progress to choose partners in any new relationship, who have also learned. Similarly, those who do not learn keep generating the same outcomes. With this overview, we can move forward to the concepts that form a foundation for this chapter. These concepts provide tools to improve relationship skills. The first of these concepts to be considered here is transactional analysis.

Transactional Analysis

As people interact, the subsystems within them also interact. The shadow aspects interact. One useful way of dividing the inner parts of a person is used in *Transactional Analysis*,[2] which links to Henriques' three parts of mind cited in Chapter 4, which proposes that we all possess an inner Parent, Adult, and Child, depicted in Figure 7.2.

There is no exact correspondence here to the Dynamics of Life diagram, but there is a resonance between the primary cycle and the parent, and the shadow and the child. The cross-over point between the two becomes the adult, balancing the two in order to maintain overall coherence. The parent

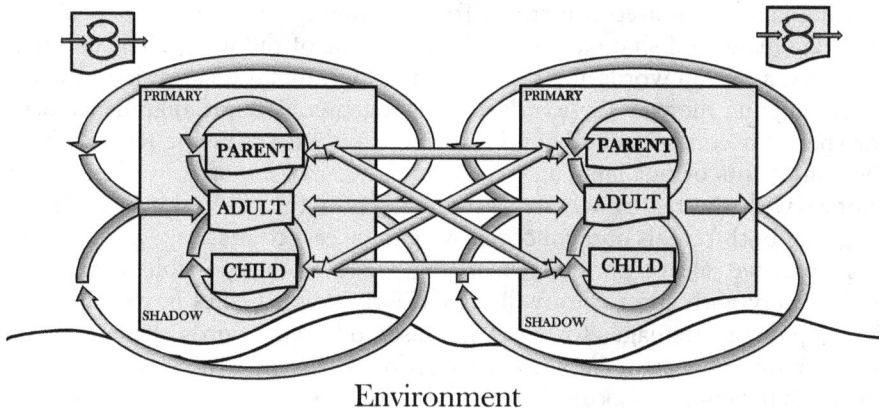

Environment

Figure 7.2 Transactional Analysis seen from within the *Dynamics of Life* model.

is the primary leader level, setting the rules and demanding compliance. The child is the rebellious shadow subsystem. The adult is the mediator, resolving the conflict and holding the coherent unity of the identity together which can become too rigid. This pattern links to Freud's superego, ego, and id.

The relationships between the three parts are in constant flux. At one time the adult is more to the fore and the others slip into the background; at other times the child or the parent comes forward.

Language

The one cognitive skill that clearly separates humans from other creatures is language. Human social capabilities skyrocketed with the invention of language, which were subsequently followed by writing, printing, and digital communication. Language opened a whole new world of ways to express feelings, discuss problems, resolve conflict, share ideas and so much more, but there is also a darker side to language. Discussion and debate can exacerbate difference, increasing conflict to the point of violence.

Claude Shannon[3] has looked at communication and noticed how it could go wrong. We can have muddled thoughts, so that we do not articulate our ideas clearly. We can speak in an imprecise manner. Similarly, there can be noises and disturbances in the environment the message moves through, and we may mishear what has been said or come to an incorrect conclusion about what the meaning of the words.

There are more than 5000 languages on the Earth, each of which has its own idiosyncratic structures. Every single language is moulded to the needs and nature of the people, and is shaped by where and how they live. The way a language is structured creates unique boundaries and categories as a way of talking about separate things, which impacts on how we make sense of our lives.

Language is a shared construct. To communicate, people must speak the same language and share a way of making sense of the world. The community must agree on words and their meanings. Grammar creates shared structures, aligning the way the words are put together. Any misalignment opens the space for confusion and conflict. We can only describe the world within the constraints of our language. As soon as we make words, we lose direct contact with the reality we are describing. As is the case with boundaries, language both reveals and conceals. We gain access to meaning-making, but as soon as we select a particular meaning, we lose other possible meanings.

A society with strict roles will have clearly defined roles in its language. The Japanese language, for instance, uses different words depending on whether one is socially superior or inferior to the person spoken to. This means that people speaking Japanese cannot talk without reinforcing their standing within the social structure. We perceive colours as a continuous range, but different cultures name colours in different ways. Some languages clearly distinguish green from blue, while others give them the same label.

Many European languages, and others such as Arabic and Hindi, distinguish gender for all nouns. Many have masculine, feminine and neuter, while French, Spanish, and Hebrew, for example, only employ masculine and feminine. In these languages, a tree, a chair, a cloud, or any other object has a gender. When the Hebrew people came to believe in a single God, that God had to be given a gender, or they could not talk about him. Given the patriarchal nature of their society, it was only natural for God to be conceived as male. Patriarchal societies tend to have languages where masculine is the default gender, with mixed groups taking masculine forms and feminine forms being created by adding an ending to the male word.

As we become more aware of the impact of language on culture, we are developing more neutral terms that are helping to make language more inclusive. "Chairman", for instance, is now more commonly replaced by "chairperson" or "chair", and humanity is commonly used where "man" was formerly used. Often names with a pejorative meaning about an outside group have been incorporated into the language. The way language has a subtle impact on how we perceive and understand our world has become largely unconscious, blinding us to the oppression hidden in our everyday words.

We see that culture creates language, but it is also true that language creates culture. Once a language is formed it alters the way the users of that language perceive the world in which they live. In Russian, the word *krasny* means both red and beautiful. It is perhaps little wonder that the communists chose red as the colour for their flag. In Japanese, the word difference is *chigau*, which is connected to the word *machigau* or *chigai*, meaning wrong. Therefore, describing a difference automatically implies being wrong. Japanese also drops pronouns (I, me, you he etc.) much more often than English, so English constantly reminds us of our separateness from others, echoing our more individualistic lifestyles.

Metaphors are central to the meaning of language, but these also change between languages. In a speech to capitalist nations in Moscow in 1956, for example, Nikita Khrushchev stated, "We will bury you", which caused outrage. Western nations took this to mean, we will kill you, whereas from a Russian perspective, it meant, "We will outlive you". The degree to which language and culture influence each other remains a hotly contested issue. Language always evolves in alignment with the rule set guiding any group.

Passive Assertive Aggressive

Any action a person undertakes will fit somewhere on a continuum between passive and aggressive. The aggressive person invades the boundaries of others and passive people have boundaries invaded. An aggressive response is rarely effective. Either the other person escalates the aggression, or they withdraw. The focus of an aggressive response is "I WIN, YOU LOSE", where the aggressor's desires are achieved at the expense of the other. The passive person, on the other hand, wishes to avoid conflict by denying their own needs. The focus here is "YOU WIN, I LOSE". A passive response may appear effective for a time because peace seems to be maintained, but it is at a cost that eventually becomes unbearable. Often passive people eventually explode to become an aggressor.

Partway along the continuum from the centre towards aggression is a position that might be called "pushy". This is where a person stands up for themselves respectfully as an autonomous person with their own views and needs. To move beyond pushy into aggressiveness becomes increasingly ineffective.

As we move from the centre towards the passive end of the continuum, there is a point we might call "tolerant". This point accepts that people are different and that we cannot always have what we want. Again, moving beyond tolerance towards passivity leads to a decrease in effectiveness. The best response is, therefore, to remain between the limits of being pushy and tolerant. This zone is called "assertiveness". The hallmark of the assertive zone is the focus on "WE WIN".

Behaviours witnessed when a person is assertive are a focus on mutual solutions, respect, politeness, remaining calm and non-judgemental, willingness to collaborate, and empathy. This is never guaranteed to resolve difference, but we can always know we did our best to offer the other person a viable pathway to the healthy resolution of difference. Even the best of us succumb to times of passivity or aggression, but as long as neither becomes an entrenched pattern of behaviour, we remain effective in our relationships.

There is a further position called "passive-aggressive". This is just another form of aggression. Passive-aggressive behaviour is never what it seems. Purely aggressive behaviour is obvious and visible. It is hidden, deniable, and sneaky. It takes many forms including talking behind people's backs, betraying confidences, lying, cynicism, hostile humour, not keeping promises, sarcasm, sulking, refusing to communicate, and getting back at people.

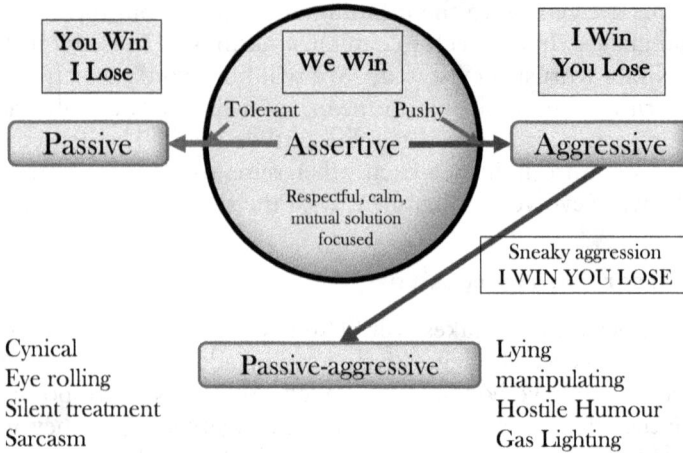

Figure 7.3 Passive or aggressive behaviour is not effective, but the middle ground of assertiveness is. Beware of passive-aggressive behaviour that can appear to be assertive.

Passive-aggressive behaviour can look like it is assertive, but the way to tell is by looking at the focus. Is it "WE WIN" or is it "I WIN", as just another form of aggression? Figure 7.3 summarises these concepts. Now you know what to look for, you will see these behaviours all around you.

The Drama Triangle and the Winner's Triangle

In the early days of research into family therapy systems, psychiatrist Murray Bowen noticed that two people in conflict only have each other to pass the hot potato between. Accordingly, a third person ends up being drawn in, either because this is at the request of one of the parties or because they actively choose to become involved. These triadic relationships can be either healthy or unhealthy. Stephen Karpman[4] depicted the unhealthy relationship in "The Drama Triangle", in which the players depicted are the persecutor, the victim, and the rescuer (Figure 7.4a).

The persecutor tries to use aggression and manipulation to force others to do as they want. Often the bravado of the persecutor is hidden by fears of inferiority, so they can easily switch to become the victim if called out. The persecutor needs a scapegoat to pay the price for what the persecutor is unwilling to take responsibility for.

Here the victim is not the victim in the sense of someone who is genuinely being abused, but rather the person who chooses to see themselves as lacking the power to change their situation. There is always someone to blame rather than being willing to take responsibility. They dodge the need to stand courageously. The victim can become enraged at their victimhood and, instead of taking an assertive stand, they may swap roles and become the persecutor.

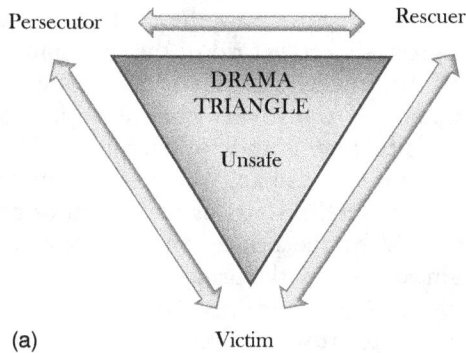

(a)   Victim

Figure 7.4a Karpman's drama triangle.   Copyright © 1967, 2008, 2020 by Stephen B. Karpman, M.D. All rights reserved for Drama Triangle, Karpman Triangle, Karpman Drama Triangle, and KarpmanDramaTriangle.com and similarities. See karpmandramatriangle.com. Used with permission of Stephen Karpman.

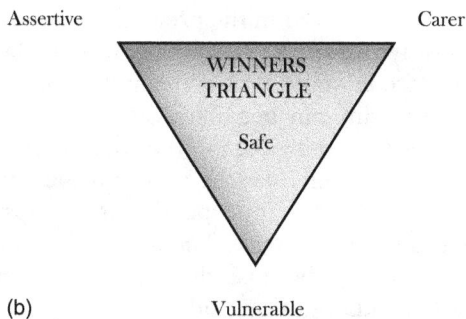

(b)   Vulnerable

Figure 7.4b The winner's Triangle formulated by Acey Choy. (From Choy, A. 1990. The Winner's Triangle. Transactional Analysis Journal, 20(1), 40-46. https://doi.org/10.1177/036215379002000105)

The persecutor and victim can unconsciously recognise and choose each other to play the game.

The rescuer may be invited by the persecutor or victim or they may move to include themselves in the game. Since it is a drama triangle, the rescuer also enters with their own agenda. Often, they feel good by being seen as the knight in shining armour, who comes to the rescue. The rescuer can hold the moral high ground, in their minds at least. If the persecutor and victim resolve their differences, the rescuer is left without any role and thus they may sabotage the situation to spark another round of drama. The victim often becomes overly reliant on the rescuer.

Each player tries to gain power in the dynamics by distorting the balance. As soon as their role does not achieve what they want, they change to another role. Roles can swap very quickly. The drama arises from the role changes.

Karpman uses fairy tales to show how the triangle works. The Pied Piper starts as the rescuer promising to get rid of the rats, and then persecutes the rats. He becomes the victim when the mayor does not give him his fee, so he responds as a persecutor of the town's children. Little Red Riding Hood begins as the rescuer visiting her grandmother, but becomes the victim of the wolf. She is rescued by the woodsman, who rescues Little Red Riding Hood and her grandmother. Cinderella starts as the victim of her stepmother and sisters, but she is rescued by the prince. She is persecuted at the stroke of midnight, but is again rescued by the prince.

It is surprising how quickly unhealthy dynamics can become accepted as "normal". Those involved grow uncomfortable without conflict and will manufacture a conflict to bring the dynamics back to the chaos that has become familiar. All three are passing the hot potato. At its worst, those involved become stuck in a feedback loop which gets worse and worse until the triangle disintegrates.

The second triangle is the "winner's triangle", formulated by Acey Choy.[5] It is sometimes referred to as the "equality triangle". Here the perpetrator becomes assertive, as we observed in the previous section. They stand up for themselves, but in positive affirming ways that cause no harm to others. This gives the victim the space to stand up for themselves and take responsibility for their actions. The victim can become assertive too, but here the word *vulnerable* is used to describe the victim in the equality triangle. The equality triangle is a safe triangle that enables the person to be vulnerable and show their weaknesses, building trust that deepens relationships. To be vulnerable in the drama triangle is to invite abuse. The rescuer becomes the carer in the equality triangle, only helping because they can, and focusing on solutions without any personal agenda or taking sides.

The winner's triangle can drift into the drama triangle. This can occur quickly, but it is more typically a slow, imperceptible drift that becomes normalised. Any one of the three participants slipping from the winner's triangle can drag all three back to the drama triangle.

Equally, however, any one of the three noticing the drift can pull the drama triangle back to the winner's triangle. If you watch people's interactions around you, you will readily see examples of Karpman's triangle. If you see it in yourself or others, you have the tools to resurrect the winner's triangle. Bowen Family Therapy discussed in the next chapter also explores triadic relationships, while John and Julie Gottman follows with his explorations of intimate partner relationships.

John and Julie Gottman

John and Julie Gottman have been researching partner relationships and working with couples for over 30 years.[6] Their ideas fit well with systems principles that shed light on relationship dynamics. While the two people in a relationship still see themselves as being "on the same team", there is a good chance that if they did genuinely work together, the relationship might be repaired and healed. One partner may think, "What you did really hurt me. It was wrong and I was harmed by it, but at the end of the day we're on the same team. We can work together to resolve our differences". Given such willingness, a path to healing remains viable. This can easily slip from "We are on the same team", to "You are the cause of the problems in this relationship". Instead of acknowledging and accepting the hot potato for what it is, it is rejected and passed on. When this happens, a tipping point is reached that is very hard to pull back from.

The Gottmans also talk about the dangers of harsh start-ups. An initial harsh start to a conversation sets the tone for the whole exchange. It is worth stopping to consider how to better start a conversation to increase the chances that it will turn out positively.

They further notice that long-term successful relationships have a way of repairing conflict that arises from time to time. Just as we should not ignore a rattle in our car or leave housework undone indefinitely, we should work to repair damage to a relationship.

The Four Horsemen

John Gottman writes of four commonly observed behaviours when a relationship is at risk of breaking up. He calls these the "Four Horsemen of the Apocalypse", a name taken from the vision of John described in Revelations, the final book of the Bible. In his vision, John foresaw the End of Days when four horsemen rode out, killing and destroying everything they encountered. Similarly, Gottman remarks that the four behaviours ride out at the end times of a relationship.

In relationships, the first horseman is *criticism*. The antidote for criticism is making a complaint. Criticism is an attack on the person, so the problem is viewed as a defect in the person's character. The antidote is to make a complaint. The focus of a complaint is the issue at hand and finding a mutual solution. A person is more likely to respond well to a complaint. Think here of how you would politely return a defective item to a shop seeking a remedy.

The second horseman is *contempt*, where we have a sense of superiority over the other person. John Gottman calls this the killer of relationships, and it is a strong indicator of a relationship at risk. The other person is seen as having less value or importance. Having contempt for someone tends to set the ground for abuse or even violence. The antidote is to have respect. When we respect someone, even if we disagree, we consider them as an equal, valid human being.

The third horseman is *defensiveness*. This is where a person is unwilling or unable to take responsibility for their actions. They make excuses or avoid the problem. Often proving "I am right" becomes more important than finding the best outcome. The antidote to defensiveness is therefore taking responsibility for our actions. A useful question to keep in mind is "What can I do that will create the best outcome for everyone?"

That does not mean we must agree to any allegation made against us, but they should be reasonably considered. Even if we acknowledge a small part of what is mentioned, a pathway is opened to a dialogue that might bridge the gap towards a suitable resolution.

That leads to the final horseman of *stonewalling*. This occurs when the people involved stop communicating. This may be a deliberate policy, employed because the person knows that silence will provoke the other person. More commonly, however, the intention is to avoid strife. There are certainly times when holding one's tongue is wise counsel. We do not have to say everything that comes to our mind, or that we might feel like saying.

The problem with remaining quiet is, first, that the stonewalling escalates tension, and, second, that since relationships are held together by communication, the pathway to healing is closed off. As hard as it may be, the antidote is to take a break, calm down and return to the issue at a later time. Gottman notes that 85% of stonewallers are men and that often stonewalling arises after the other three horsemen are already apparent.

Even in the best of partnerships, now and then one of the four horsemen will arise. A comment will be unnecessarily sharp or attacking, and a partner will go quiet or whatever, but when it becomes an entrenched pattern, it becomes a sign to watch out for if the relationship is to be rescued.

Key Points

1 When two people meet, all the levels and sublevels interact simultaneously.
2 Language is the key tool we use to communicate. Different languages reflect their culture through the distinctions they make in their language.
3 Cultures form shared rule sets to create common understandings but when different cultures and languages conflict problems may arise.
4 Any behaviour sits on a continuum between passive and aggressive. The middle ground of assertiveness is the best place to be. Beware of being passive-aggressive.
5 Stephen Karpman recognised three-person interactions in the drama triangle or the equality triangle.
6 John Gottman tells us to avoid harsh start-ups and to beware of the Four Horsemen of the Apocalypse – four behaviours that foretell the end of days for a relationship: criticism, contempt, defensiveness, and stonewalling.

Notes

1 See *The Witch and the Clown* by Barry and Ann Ulanov.
2 See *Transactional Analysis in Psychotherapy: A Systematic Individual and Social Psychiatry* by Eric Berne.

3 See *A Mathematical Theory of Communication* by Claude Shannon.
4 See *A Game Free Life: The New Transactional Analysis of Intimacy, Openness, and Happiness* by Stephen Karpman. Thanks to Stephen Karpman for his suggestions about writing this section.
5 See Choy, A. (1990). The Winner's Triangle. *Transactional Analysis Journal*, 20(1), 40–46. https://doi.org/10.1177/036215379002000105 permission from Copyright Clearance Centre 1513541.
6 See *The Relationship Cure: A Five-Step Guide to Strengthening your Marriage, Family and Relationships* by John and Julie Gottman.

Bibliography

Berne, E. (2015). Transactional Analysis in psychotherapy: A systematic individual and social psychiatry. Martino Fine books. https://books.google.co.nz/books?hl=en&lr=&id=hYjjDAAAQBAJ&oi=fnd&pg=PT8&dq=eric+berne+transactional+analysis&ots=1Fu1SLVzKC&sig=Dv_EWMqg_4sXqMqHEVmauH37Y_c#v=onepage&q=eric+berne+transactional+analysis&f=false

Choy, A. (1990). The Winner's Triangle. *Journal of Transactional Analysis*, 20(1), 40–46.

Gottman, J., & DeClaire, J. (2001). *The Relationship Cure: A Five Step Guide to Strengthening Your Marriage, Family and Relationships*. Three Rivers Press.

Gottman, J., & Gottman, J. (2015). Gottman Couple Theory. In A. Gurman, J. Lebow Douglas, & K. Snyder (Eds.), *Clinical Handbook of Couple Therapy* (5th edition). Guilford Press.

Gottman, J., & Silver, N. (2015). *The Seven Principles for Making Marriage Work (Issue 1999)*. Harmony.

Karpman, S. (1968). Fairy Tale and Script Drama Analysis. *Transactional Analysis Journal*, 7(26), 39–43.

Karpman, S. (2019). *Collected Papers in Transactional Analysis*. Drama Triangle Publications.

Karpman, S. B. (2014). *A Game Free Life: The New Transactional Analysis of Intimacy, Openness, and Happiness* (First Edition). Drama Triangle Publications.

Shannon, C. (1948). A Mathematical Theory of Communication. The *Bell System Technical Journal*, 27(July, October), 379–423, 623–656. http://cm.bell-labs.com/cm/ms/what/shannonday/shannon1948.pdf

Ulanov, A., & Ulanov, B. (1987). *The Witch and the Clown: Two Archetypes of Human Sexuality*. Chiron Publishers. http://www.amazon.com/The-Witch-Clown-Archetypes-Sexuality/dp/0933029071

Chapter 8

Further Concepts and Strategies

Introduction

As we delve deeper into human social dynamics, we develop a greater understanding of tensions and trade-offs and how they play out in our lives. This chapter continues builds on the concepts presented in the last chapter, which was more focused on intimate partner relationships. These are expanded in this chapter to include family dynamics.

Time Out

Time Out is a powerful strategy when the dynamics of a relationship have reached boiling point. If a person is at a 6 on the Anger Scale mentioned in Chapter 5, 'Angry but still in control', but is still moving up the scale, then it is appropriate to call a Time Out from the partner. There are six steps to follow that help make it more likely that taking a Time Out will be effective.

1 A plan needs to be agreed between both partners when everyone is calm and relaxed, before a Time Out is needed. The plan will include what the person will do during the Time Out, where they will go, and how long they will absent themselves for. Two potential problems can be avoided by having a plan. The first is the other person not allowing the Time Out. To them, calling a Time Out is just an excuse to avoid the issue, and this can indeed be the case. A true Time Out enables a respectful dialogue that is more likely to resolve the issue.

The second problem is the fear of what the person will do once they have left. Will they get drunk and return in a violent state? Will they visit a previous partner, or will they not come back? This fear is hopefully allayed by having an agreement about what will happen in the Time Out before one is needed.

DOI: 10.4324/9781003533641-8

2 When a Time Out is needed, it can happen quickly and easily because a plan is already in place. The person just needs to say, "I need to take a time out." At this point all the agreements automatically kick in.

3 It is important to do something positive when taking time out. Going for a run, a bike ride, or walking the dog are all such examples. Exercise reduces adrenaline and cortisol levels, and calms the person. Vigorous exercise can help as long as you retain a positive mental state. Talking to someone you both trust can be helpful as they will give positive advice and not escalate the situation. Other distracting behaviours, such as a hobby, music, or watching television or a video, can help you calm down.

There are four D's to avoid: drinking, drugs, driving, and dangerous activities. Sometimes driving is necessary to escape a situation but since an angry person is more likely to drive faster and take risks, particular care should be taken in such a situation. Chopping wood or working in the garage with power tools can also be dangerous.

4 After the agreed time, make contact by either phone or text. It takes a minimum of 20 minutes for adrenaline to subside in the body, so a break of an hour is probably good. First, just check in, so either of you can request more time to settle and calm down further if needed.

5 When both are agreed, return. When a fire has died down to a few embers, it looks like it is out, but putting a log on it can cause it to reignite immediately. It is best not to discuss the issue straight away in case it flares up again.

6 Organise a time to talk, perhaps the next day, when everyone is calm. That also gives everyone time to think about what happened and the best way to set up the conversation. It may be a good idea to introduce a third person, who can help the discussion.

The issue must ultimately be discussed and resolved, or trust may be lost for the next time a Time Out is called. If it has gone well, it is much easier to call a Time Out on the next occasion.

Moving Towards, Away, and Against

Karen Horney[1] (pronounced *horn-eye*) proposed that when we experienced distressing or traumatic situations while young, we unconsciously selected one of three ways to respond that we generally continue to use into adulthood. Each of the three ways has both a positive and a negative expression as in Table 8.1.

The child who *moves towards* the caregiver hopes that by engaging they will meet their needs. If this is done well and the caregiver responds, the child will bond and learn skills of connecting with others and building healthy relationships. Because they feel safe and protected, they are not disturbed when the caregiver is absent. When moving towards is expressed in unhelpful ways, it appears as co-dependence and needy behaviour. The child becomes

Table 8.1 Karen Horney's moving towards, moving away, and moving against

Movement	Positive expression	Negative expression	Need
Move towards	Learn to build relationships and positive bonding	Co-dependent, needy, clingy	Love Connection
Move away	Learn to be self-sufficient	Isolated and withdrawn	Power
Move against	Learn to place boundaries to stay safe	Abuse, bullying and violence	Autonomy/ Freedom

clingy and unwilling to leave the caregiver, and becomes distressed when the caregiver is not present. The risk for a moving towards child is that they suppress emotion to become a "good" boy or girl and become too compliant.

Other children *move away*. They think that if the caregiver does not meet their needs, they will become self-reliant and satisfy their own needs. The positive side of this is that it builds skills of independence and self-sufficiency but when it becomes negative, the child withdraws to become isolated and suspicious of others. They do not learn the skills of engaging. The moving away child avoids rejection by not interacting.

Finally, the child may *move against*, meaning that they rebel and try to force others to meet their needs. When positive, this leads to assertive boundary setting. When dysfunctional, it manifests as aggressive, abusive, and even violent behaviour, making the other do what they desire. The moving away child passes the hot potato and avoids taking responsibility for their actions.

Karen Horney notes that each individual will use one of the three as their primary styles. When that fails, however, we can each adopt a second backup style. It can be enlightening to compare your styles with those of your partner. This may help to explain some of the dynamics in your relationship. We might choose a partner whose main style is the one we have not chosen, in an unconscious attempt to develop what we perceive as our weaker style to a more mature state. Karen Horney stated that the goal for a mature adult is to express the positive aspects of all three approaches in a balanced way. In the next section we will consider another approach. Whereas Karen Horney focused on behavioural styles, Robert Kegan sought to understand life phases.

Robert Kegan and Empathy

Robert Kegan[2] notes that, in broad terms, we develop through stages from a baby to a child to an adolescent to a mature adult, which can be linked to the life, mind, and social layers. More recently, he has been writing more about these levels as a network rather than a linear progression.

When we reach a new level, our understanding is unconscious and must be learned. All levels exist from birth in a nascent form and they then become activated at the right time. Over time, we become conscious of our experience at the new level and come to act with awareness and skill.

A newborn baby is not conscious of its body. It simply experiences sounds, shapes, sights, smells, etc. It must learn to appreciate its body as being separate from the world. Over time, it gains conscious control of its body. A toddler experiences emotions in an unconscious manner, resulting in tantrums and difficult behaviours. Emotions become conscious and more controlled. For example, the toddler has good control of their body. Several years later, logical thinking is experienced unconsciously and becomes conscious. Emotions become stabilised, and the body is well controlled.

The next step is the social level, reached in the teenage years, recognising other people in their lives. The baby and child knew there were others in their world and relied on them, but the focus was always on themselves. Teenagers take several years to move beyond their self-obsession. Building relationships with others occurs in a series of steps as the social self becomes increasingly conscious.

Empathy

In childhood, we focus on ourselves and our own needs. We come to realise that we cannot achieve all we want by ourselves. The first level of empathy is making friends with others so we can meet our own needs. At this stage as soon as there is no longer a need to be met, there is no need for the friendship. Alcoholics and drug addicts can carry this stage well into adult life. As long as someone supplies them with their addictions, they will be friends; as soon as that stops or they place demands on them, however, the relationship ends. Teenagers tend to gather in small groups and are very conscious of who is in and who is out. As we mature, we can form genuine relationships with a widening range of people. At a spiritual level, we have love for everyone, even our enemies. As we mature, we include others increasingly into our lives and build empathy. We also develop self-authorship to become who we truly feel ourselves to be rather than being defined by others.

We can understand empathy from another angle. Before empathy comes sympathy. In the past, I have fallen and hurt myself. When I see someone else fall over, I remember my falling, but sympathy is a detached sense of knowing that assumes all people are like me. It is an "Oh dear, poor you, that must have been terrible!" response.

The next step in this process is empathy, which occurs when we genuinely feel what an experience might be like for someone else. We have neurons in our brain, called mirror neurons, that fire when we watch somebody do something, that trigger the same neural pathways as though it were happening to us. We have a physical feeling in our body that mirrors what is happening to the person. If I stand by a cliff, I get tingling calves. If I watch someone stand near a cliff face, I will also get tingly calves. People wince in pain when they notice something painful happening to others. The Dalai Lama believes a further step from empathy is compassion, when we choose to act to help the person we have empathy for.

Different people can have very different experiences of the same situation. Two people sit next to each other on a roller coaster. Both feel the same physical sensations, but one is ecstatic and the other terrified. At this point it is useful to work through an example. A man comes home drunk, but not so drunk that he does not know what he is doing. His partner had a meal ready which is now cold, and she is angry. An argument starts and they begin pushing each other. There are several other people in the room.

A one-year-old baby in the room would feel distress, but would not understand this experience, making it more distressing. They could only cry to try and change the situation. Similarly, a nine-year-old would understand the words but not really understand the dynamics. They could run out of the room or call out. The feelings of discomfort and lack of safety are still intense, however. They understand what is happening better than the one-year-old.

A sixteen-year-old would typically overestimate their understanding. They might even intervene physically or verbally. They would feel the pressure to take sides and thus feel torn between the two principal people in their lives. While still traumatic and uncomfortable, they would usually feel safer than either the nine-year-old or one-year-old.

Depending on their mental and physical capabilities, an eighty-year-old in the room will understand the dynamics and may have wise words to offer, but they would feel vulnerable. Their focus would also tend to be on others in the room.

The drunk man is likely to be self-absorbed and fail to notice the impact of his actions. He will not have any concerns about his safety. He is the person in the room with the greatest ability to change what is happening and make everyone safe.

The woman feels angry. Her past experience of the man coming home drunk will be at the forefront of her mind. She is likely to be thinking of the welfare of others in the room as well as her own, but fear will build as emotions intensify. She knows that if the situation becomes physical, she will almost certainly end up worse off, causing her to measure how much emotion she can show before it becomes dangerous.

Table 8.2 shows a generalised view of types of people. There are, of course, enormous variations in the skills and behaviours for each category. We can think of many more variables that would have an impact on how a person might experience the situation, such as physical stature, fitness, culture, cognitive abilities, disabilities, religious beliefs, and so forth, but the purpose of the story is to make the point that different people can experience the same event very differently.

A person who is empathic and aware of these differences, and is thoughtful about how to interact with people, will have a more effective range of responses to any particular situation. As an example, the thought of walking two kilometres at 2 a.m. in an area where there is no good street lighting

Table 8.2 Different people experience the same event in different ways

	Understanding	Power to act	Safety	Focus
1-year-old	Low	Cry	Low	Self
9-year-old	Low-Moderate	Cry, talk	Low	Self
16-year-old	High-Moderate	Intervene	Moderate	Self and others
80-year-old	High	Add wisdom	Low-Moderate	Self and others
Man	High	Most power to change	High	Self
Woman	High	Persuasion	Low-Moderate	Self and others

would not be seen as particularly scary or problematic for most men. That same situation for a woman is likely to generate fear and concern. It encourages us to build on our skills of recognising differences between us and others and the impact that has on their experience of any situation so we can better respond to their needs. It also helps me be aware of my impact on others.

If someone does something that I consider abhorrent, wrong, harmful, or evil, it can be useful to reconsider my understanding of them and their past. That does not alter their responsibility for their actions or stop me from acting as I see I need to reduce harm or maintain my own sense of integrity, but it does open the pathway for a deeper understanding of why people act as they do and increases my range of responses. It is often said that "Hurt people hurt people". Broadening our empathic skills allows us to respond more effectively, rather than just responding to the other out of habit.

Bowen Family System Theory

In the late 1960s Murray Bowen[3] developed a way of working with whole families. In many ways, it was a reaction to the predominant individualistic approach to counselling. Bowen claims a client needs to be considered within the context of the environment in which they live. He saw family members taking up roles played out through recursive interactions. Much of the original work, at least, is couched in terms of the psychological understandings of the 1960s. It privileges rational thinking, so a 4e cognition approach would help update Bowen's idea. He also tends to see the therapist as being outside the family system, rather than acknowledging their impact on the family dynamics. Bowen saw the role of family members as differentiating themselves as individuals, linking to Maslow's self-actualised person as the top level of development, but it is caught in Western thinking. Indigenous cultures would see someone integrated into their community as more evolved than an individual only integrated in themselves. Nevertheless, he made a valuable contribution towards a way of working with people in a more systems-based way.

As we have seen from the *Dynamics of Life* model, energy, matter, and information move through family systems. As family members experience each other, anxiety arises when events are difficult for family members to resolve, and they tend to pass on the hot potato in the form of their anxiety to others. Patterns of coping are co-created by those involved. We explore some of Bowen's concepts.

Family Projection Process

When a couple comes together, they pass their emotional energy back and forth. When children are born, that emotional energy must be shared between the partner and the child. This can easily be perceived as a loss and missing out on emotional energy. The family passes the hot potato. The child could feel deprived if the parents are too absorbed in each other.

Commonly, a family will recognise their weakest link and that person becomes the dumping ground for unresolved family conflict. They become the black sheep. Rather than family members recognising and acknowledging their actions, they betray the family member by scapegoating and dumping the chaos they cannot handle onto them.

Sibling Birth Order

Bowen wrote extensively about the impact of birth order. The firstborn tends to be doted on and have high expectations placed on them. They must be self-reliant and shoulder responsibility. If the parents are not fulfilling their role as a parent, it can fall on the oldest to pick up the role. Middle-born children have an older sibling to help. They are brought up having to share and get on with others. The lastborn is often spoilt. They have the most extreme experience of having to share and get along with a larger number of siblings. They can learn to expect things to be done for them. The gaps in age between the siblings and the genders also make a difference. Often sons and daughters are treated differently. If there is one boy amongst several girls or one girl amongst boys, the dynamics are altered once again.

Parents can separate, breaking the family apart and perhaps, later, blending with other families. Children may live away from their families through a variety of circumstances: illness, immigration, war, death, and many others.

Intergenerational Effects

What one generation cannot process is passed on to the next, and some effects cascade down the generations. The trauma of war, starvation, pandemics, and natural disasters can all have effects that last beyond one generation.

People tend to seek out partners with a similar level of differentiation to themselves and import their patterns of behaving from their family of origin. Bowen noted that dysfunction in one generation can be amplified as it moves down the generations, sometimes resulting in a schizophrenic child. The first son of the first son, or the first daughter of the first daughter, often feels the pressure even more than an ordinary firstborn.

This highlights the value of exploring family history or whakapapa, which is the Māori term. It is interesting to have information on the lives of our ancestors, but it is even more useful to explore the intergenerational dynamics within families to help identify patterns that might be unconsciously impacting on our behaviour.

Key Points

1 Time Out is an excellent strategy when a situation is about to boil over.
2 Karen Horney says that as children we choose to move towards others, move away, or move against. Each path has both its positive expression and its negative expression.
3 Robert Kegan says new skills are unconscious at first, but that over time they become conscious.
4 Empathy is a critical learnable social skill. First, we compare others to ourselves, but later we recognise how their experience might be different from ours.
5 Murray Bowen developed the system of Bowen Family Therapy. He notices how family members project their anxiety on other family members. He also stresses sibling birth order and intergenerational effects.

Notes

1 See *Neurosis and Human Growth: The Struggle Towards Self Realization* by Karen Horney.
2 See *The Evolving Self: Problem and Process in Human Development* by Robert Kegan.
3 See *The Eight Concepts of Bowen Therapy* by Roberta Gilbert.

Bibliography

Gilbert, R., & Jacobs, G. (2018). *The Eight Concepts of Bowen Theory* (1st edition). Leading Systems Press. https://www.amazon.com.au/Eight-Concepts-Bowen-Theory/dp/097634551X

Horney, K. (1991). *Neurosis and Human Growth: The Struggle Toward Self-Realization* (2nd edition). W W Norton and Company.

Kegan, R. (2009). *The Evolving Self: Problem and Process in Human Development* (Reprint edition). Harvard University Press. https://www.amazon.com/gp/product/B003772KJC/ref=dbs_a_def_rwt_hsch_vapi_tkin_p1_i3

Chapter 9

Culture and Community

Introduction

In many animals and early human societies, brute strength was often the way someone improved their power and fitness to survive. Many animal species have an alpha male, who often gains much of the group's compliance through fear. When we evolved to the psychological level, social influence took over as the pathway to increase fitness. Instead of controlling people's bodies, power is more typically exercised by controlling social perceptions and social reputations. Building social alliances, rhetorical skills, persuading others, political strategies, and developing charisma became more important. Social influence can be used in positive, supportive ways or through creating division and discord.

Social evolution greatly increased our capacity to cooperate and develop a global society. For good and bad, our new technologies arose out of social cooperation. This chapter explores this development over the millennia and suggests some ways we may learn to reconnect as societies and live beyond violence. We start by again exploring ideas and introducing new concepts.

What is a Human Being?

A human being simultaneously operates at the life, mind, cultural, and spiritual levels. Within the biological life level, we are a collection of trillions of cells, tissues, body organs, and body systems all collaborating. The psychological level of mind includes many conscious and unconscious forces interacting. Ideas and concepts build upon each other to form coherent sense-making structures. At the cultural social level, our complex social arrangements enable collaboration.

The higher the level of brain functioning, the easier it is to change them. At the social level, we have conventions that are true because we all choose to believe them, but those conventions change over time. Homosexuality was a crime, but now it is mostly an accepted part of life. At the lower levels of brain function, we have less power to change them. While much of our

DOI: 10.4324/9781003533641-9

male and female nature is socially proscribed, some is biological. It is encoded in our genes. That is much harder to change and therefore more likely to be a constraint we must learn to live with. Men, for example, are more likely to use physical violence.[1] That cannot be changed by working only at the social level.

We respond not only to physical threats but to anything that might threaten our social position, whether it is for a mate, more resources, or power. Fitness in our lived environment has shifted from being derived from physical prowess to social reputation. If I can influence other people to act as I would like, I gain social power. We have evolved social emotions to equip us to compete for influence and power. We have ambition, envy, jealousy, injustice, greed, shame, guilt, and more. We are primed to strive to increase social influence.

Each level, and all its subsystem levels, are fractally conjoined and impact each other. They are maps of each other. Our social maps are the basis of culture. Culture arises from the shared agreements of people about what is acceptable and what is unacceptable. Some of our mapping is enshrined in law, while other parts are implicit. We have ways to set a table, form queues for fairness, and smile as we pass people on the street. Culture is prone to error. Those who rise to the top of a social hierarchy often have an investment to stay there and manipulate and marginalise others.

This all fits within a wider environment and spiritual connectedness. We truly are a marvel, and it is easy to see why we would be described as the image of the living God, but we also embody the paradox of the inherent error that leads to abuse and violence at all levels of life.

Causal Layered Analysis

We tend to simplify complex situations to create single linear solutions. We think if we just fix the one thing that is wrong, all will be well. That rarely happens. Causal Layered Analysis (CLA) was formulated by Sohail Inayatullah to ensure that any situation is examined from a range of perspectives.[2] CLA offers a comprehensive overview of a situation to see how an intervention at any one level might impact the whole situation.

Inayatullah often presents CLA as an iceberg because only the top layer of the iceberg is visible. We see this in Figure 9.1. We only become aware of lower levels when we seek them. As we go through the layers you will see the links to our *Dynamics of Life* model, especially regarding rule sets.

The top layer is called *litany*. This is the level of everyday interactions. Inayatullah cites the example of a newspaper headline that only gives the basic outline with no nuance or detail. It is the mode we are in when we go to the supermarket, fill up with petrol, or undertake any everyday tasks.

Sitting beneath that is the *systemic* layer. This should not be confused with the way we use the word systems in this book. By systems, Inayatullah means the social rules, conventions, and how daily life is organised. We use these

Causal Layered Analysis

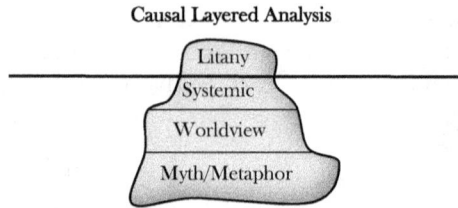

Figure 9.1 The Causal Layered Analysis model with the litany visible above the surface, but the systems, worldview, and myth/metaphor level beneath the surface form the foundation.   Reprinted with permission of Sohail Inayatullah.

rules in our daily tasks at the litany level. This includes how various agencies and social functions in our society are organised. There are local bylaws, state laws, and national laws we must all obey. Our lives are shaped by the cultural agreements written and unwritten that we abide by.

The layer below the systems layer is the *worldview*. This is an internally consistent narrative about how to see the world and make sense of experience. It is a shared story defining the cohesive ideas holding a group of people together. The systems layer is the expression of the worldview in action just as the *litany* is the expression of the systems layer.

The deepest layer is the *myth/metaphor* layer, which is the core image or story from which the worldview unfolds. This moves us deeply into our unconscious mind, going beyond words to link to more foundational levels of sense-making that connects us all. It is the realm of archetypes and mythic characters that have constellated as shared psychological entities living at the core of our being. Whoever has control over the central metaphor has enormous power. The words we use, and the metaphors that hold them together, structure how we experience our world.

You can see how the worldview arises from the myth/metaphor layer. Each layer defines the one above it. Table 9.1 demonstrates an example of a CLA analysis.

If a society has a violent foundational metaphor, that will filter down through the levels, resulting in violence at the litany level. A patriarchal society will have patriarchal myths. Change spreads to other levels.

The layers of CLA bear a rough resemblance to the levels in the *Dynamics of Life* model. The litany of everyday life is a bit like the biological realm. The systemic causes are like the psychological level. The worldview is a coherent value and belief set that resonates with the thinking but also links to the social level because a worldview is a set of shared beliefs in a society. The myth/metaphor level is like the spiritual that transcends the practical levels of development.

Donella Meadows wrote that the deeper the level at which change is made, the more pervasive the repercussions. If we make a change at the systems level, it can influence the systems and litany levels, but will not change the

Table 9.1 Causal Layered Analysis

Causal Layered Analysis	Neo-liberal/patriarchal	Systems
Litany	Small wealthy group, masses of poor, discriminated, and marginalised people	Mutual social support in daily life, a healthy planet
Systemic/social causes	Business and social structures privatise benefits and socialise negative effects	Supportive social structures that ensure everyone has what they need; care of nature
Worldview	Money determines value, individualistic greed, separation	Connectedness between parts, mutual support
Myth/metaphor	Fat man gorging on food	A tree

overarching worldview or metaphor from which it comes. If we provide a new metaphor everything is restructured. The worldview changes to align itself and then the systems and litany levels must also align.

As in Table 9.1, we can use the CLA framework to recognise the existing structure to formulate a new metaphor that encapsulates the preferred future. Then working back level by level, we can formulate more specific details of how to implement the new vision.

Working Ethically with People

Gerald Midgley[3] has been working for many years on Critical Systems Theory, being concerned that systems theory are principles that can work to harm people as much as they can help. He has built ethical principles we ought to remain mindful of to ensure that any project operates to alert us about ways harm might be caused to stakeholders in that project. He outlines six key points that help to maintain ethical principles in any project:

1 Amplify marginalised voices
   There will almost invariably be voices that have not been fully heard. Often, they become scapegoats paying the costs for other people's actions. Ignoring those voices can result in angry backlashes.
2 Blur boundaries
   Look at the bigger picture. There are often external pressures that might impact the system and how it operates. If we are not aware of these influences, we will be confused by the way the system responds.
3 Unite with a common goal
   Sometimes when people come together over a problem it is good to focus on what they share. If it is about maintaining the cleanliness of a river, different stakeholders will have very different views, but their shared

goal can provide the necessary cohesion to overcome differences. Uniting against a common enemy can have the downside of creating conflict and violence against an external enemy.

4 Transcend narrow boundaries

If we have only looked at a problem from our own perspective, we are likely to miss important understandings. Taking other perspectives helps us recognise assumptions we took for granted and notice their impact on the project.

5 Undermine negative stereotypes; look for connections

We have a human tendency to create stereotypes. It is a simpler, more linear way of making sense that often comes to the wrong conclusion. By seeking out connections between ideas and looking at disconfirming evidence, we are more likely to reach a correct conclusion.

6 Work with all stakeholders

So often those in charge of a hierarchy plan from within their own knowledge without seeking information from others. Include all stakeholders early in the process so they feel included and empowered by the process rather than having a solution imposed upon them.

We now move to explore our social evolution through the major stages of history. Each stage saw a whole new increasingly complex way people could organise themselves. By understanding our history, we can understand why our world is shaped and structured as it is. This may help us cope with the complex social arrangements we find ourselves negotiating. You will note similarities to the Tree of Life in Chapter 3.

Structural Violence

Social organisation was the springboard to civilisation as we know it. There are inherent tensions and trade-offs that often result in abuse and violence arising not from the individuals, but from the social structure itself. All life creates hierarchies because they are effective at reducing entropy. Hierarchies necessarily create inequality and marginalisation as some people have more resources available to them.

Just as an individual has a cognitive map, we have cultural maps that define how a society interprets reality and establishes the rule set with its rewards and punishments. Those in power seek to maintain their power. Often the social structure takes on a self-perpetuating life of its own that is harmful for its members. When the utopian dream of those who took power is not realised, scapegoats are identified to pay the price others are not prepared to pay. The marginalised and scapegoated people seek justice and find ways to regain what they see as their rightful place. Sometimes this causes an overthrow of the established hierarchy, restarting the whole cycle of structural violence. In earlier social structures, physical violence maintained the people's compliance to perpetuate the social structure. But, more recently, it has been realised that controlling the guiding narrative, the worldview, is more powerful.[4] Regime change is moving from physical rebellion to media control. We have moved from cutting off heads to media control and destroying social reputations, but the underlying process is unchanged.

Johan Galtung[5] writes that cultural violence is not a direct action as such, but arises from the values and beliefs enshrined in a culture that enable abuse and violence to occur. A misguided narrative leads to misguided rule sets and thus misguided actions.

Sometimes structural violence is deliberately created to maintain power. Over time, we have seen racism, sexism, ageism, and a raft of other discriminatory practices become encoded into our social mapping just as it is in our individual cognitive mapping. They become entrenched into our social structures to the point of becoming invisible. Norms are established which exclude people or sectors of a society, who end up scapegoated to pay the price of actions caused by others. These norms can become so pervasive as to even be supported by those who suffer as a result. Structural violence creates benefits for some people, who develop a blindness to the violence to avoid the loss of the benefits, often unfairly gained. Power and privilege often perpetuate violence.

Slavery is an extreme example of structural violence that has been with us since our early days. Slavery has only relatively recently been considered abhorrent because it was previously so central to maintaining the accustomed lifestyle. The women's movement, LGBTQIA+ rights, older people's rights, and disabled people of different races have all been discriminated against throughout history and only very recently received any real recognition of the harm and violence perpetrated. We are unwilling to do what we know is needed to stop climate change because it would be too disruptive to our lifestyle. It leaves us all wondering what our descendants will make of our behaviours and which actions we take for granted will horrify them.

Human Cultures

Writing about stages of history is contentious because we so easily fall into cultural assumptions of superiority or bias. It is common, especially in the West, for people to formulate stage theories that place their own culture or worldview as the top level. There is enormous indigenous wisdom we have lost through our disconnected lifestyles. The social structure we live within is only one among many that could have evolved and many of those alternative futures could well be superior to ours. Every step of the way, shadow structures challenge the primary story.

As we examine the stages of history you will notice that each level of social evolution, from hunter-gatherer to democracy, had its own *Dynamics of Life* model playing out. They had the primary structure, shadow structure, external threats and opportunities, and their own hierarchy to manage the entropy that inevitably arose. As one level proved insufficient to contain social disorder, a new social level emerged.

Our earliest ancestors were hunter-gatherers. Life was generally simpler and egalitarian. They were a bit like the men's group we investigated earlier, not needing a complex infrastructure. Language and technologies like fire, the wheel, cooking, and tools greatly enhanced their ability to survive. With a much lower population, it was easy to shift to a new area if numbers increased or there was conflict between groups. The smaller groups would often come together in much larger groups for specific rituals or ceremonies with quite different social structures. Human societies have been able to come together in surprisingly large numbers without a complex infrastructure, but, generally, hunter-gatherers were small groups with distributed leadership.[6]

As populations grew, resources like land became scarce and agriculture arose as a more convenient way to access food.[7] Groups became tribal, living in defined territories.

It became more effective to appoint a chief to facilitate decision-making. Because they competed for resources, they had to organise themselves better than the tribes next to them or they would lose their place and the resources of that location. Living in one location led to storing food, erecting buildings, and developing arts and crafts. Now, there was a need to protect everything which required warriors. As well as protecting, warriors could be used to gain extra resources by taking over new territory. There was typically a council of elders and a shaman to guide the chief and the people and safeguard tribal wisdom and mythology that enshrined the rule set, as depicted in Figure 9.2. The tribal map defined the community. Membership was mostly by genealogical connection. Each tribe needed to clearly separate itself from neighbouring tribes, so styles of art, linguistic dialects, and signs of social rank all emerged. Neighbouring tribes were often seen as a threat. Violence, the threat of violence, or banishment remained the final source of upholding social compliance.

Over time tribes would amalgamate, join in alliances, be overtaken by conquest, or even destroyed, resulting in the emergence of empires. The tribes' separate mythologies needed to be amalgamated by a shared belief system that would tie the people together as a cohesive society. Christianity, Islam, Buddhism, and other religions arose in the time of empires to function as a uniting rule set amongst a plethora of gods within the tribes. Often older beliefs were absorbed into new belief systems. Many pagan beliefs have been woven into Christianity. They also developed uniting laws to be enforced.

New Zealand, in the time of Te Rauparaha[8] in the early 1800s, reflects a time when tribal groups joined together. Te Rauparaha decided to move from his tribal area near Raglan in the north down to *Kāpiti* Island. Tribes passed on the way had the choice of fighting him and facing annihilation, allowing him safe passage, or joining him to share the spoils. When he tried to extend

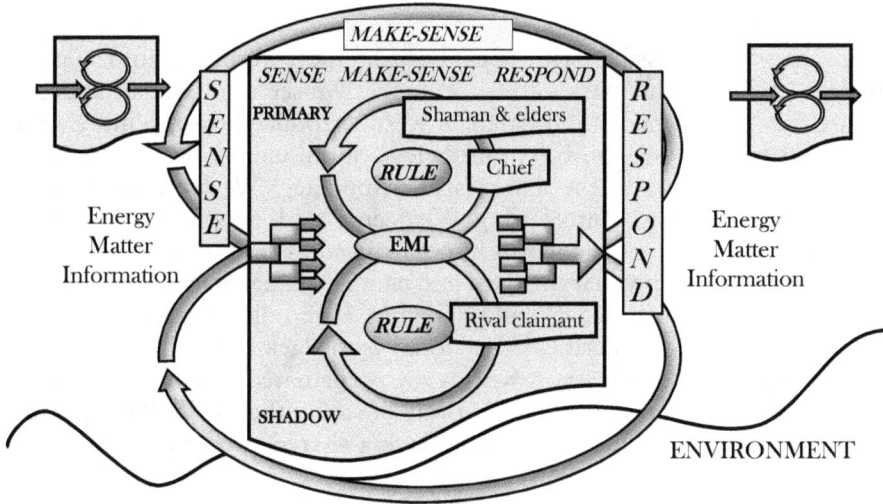

Figure 9.2 The Dynamics of Life diagram for tribal societies.

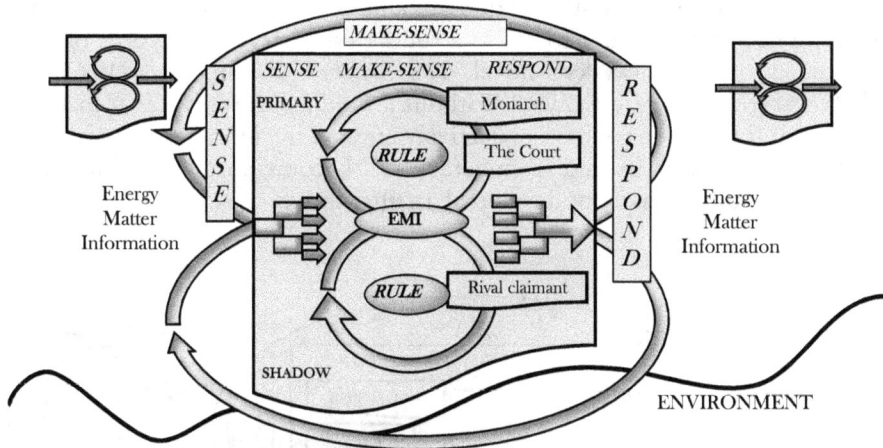

Figure 9.3 The Dynamics of Life diagram for empires.

his boundaries into the South Island, his progress was thwarted by southern tribes, but had he succeeded, he may have continued to become the first emperor of the Māori people.

Empires were ruled by emperors or monarchs, who governed by the "Divine Right of Kings", as seen in Figure 9.3. As people became literate and had access to information and more technologies, they came to see their rulers as fallible and oppressive, leading to a cascade of revolutions, overthrowing the emperors, and instituting democratic governments.

Democracy

Democracy was possible with education, literacy, access to information, and the ability of the masses to travel more. We see the basic structure in Figure 9.4. Many checks and balances were introduced to stop individuals or groups from taking control; nevertheless, our modern world has seen the breakdown of many of the markers of democracy. We see multinational corporations buying control of governments and people driven by an ideology that separates the world into parts and assigns a monetary value. People are increasingly marginalised and climate change issues loom menacingly. We have also had a global pandemic, economic instability, and the threat of nuclear war. A critical issue today is the lack of a cohesive mythology. As much as the Christian worldview perpetuated abusive and violent social structures, it provided a united way of seeing the world. We often feel lost and fragmented today because we lack a shared way of understanding our world.

Nietzsche correctly stated that "God is dead", meaning the old story told by the churches to maintain their power had been exposed. The church's narrative only had validity while people believed the stories, but Nietzsche could not produce a new story. Human beings cannot exist without a story. We have been left well out to sea in a rudderless boat. In the words of Ivan Karamazov in Dostoyevsky's novel, *The Brothers Karamazov*, "If God is dead, everything is permissible." Without a binding story, we drift lost and conflicted. It feels like we have collectively entered the insanity that overtook Nietzsche's life near its end. Democracy has become so distorted as to be unsuitable, but we have not developed an alternative.

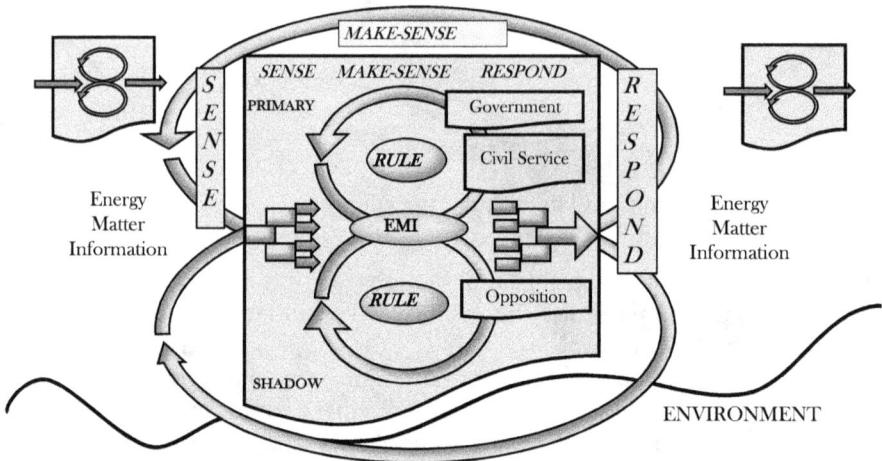

Figure 9.4 The Dynamics of Life diagram for a democracy.

While our situation looks dire, it may also be an opportunity to create new stories that make sense of the world we find ourselves in enabling another leap forward in how we organise ourselves and live our lives.

Beyond Democracy

You were born into the world with certain capabilities and predispositions, but you were shaped by the people and culture around you. You learned not only the words but also the attitudes and values, the ways of seeing the world, that fused together in your sense of identity. Culture is passed on in both good and bad ways through the generations.

The predominant paradigm most people live by today is a fractured, separated way of seeing the world. Opinions are increasingly divisive, mental health is declining, and people's whole sense of well-being is under threat. Life is increasingly precarious.

But you and I have free will to change our minds. Systems wisdom reveals a pathway to reconnect to ourselves, others, and the world in which we live. We move on in the next chapter to explore some of those alternatives that give us hope in a lost world.

Key Points

1 A human being combines the biological, psychological, and social (and spiritual) aspects all interacting at the same time, including all the subsystems.
2 Inayatullah's Causal Layered Analysis examines any situation from the litany, systems, worldview, and myth/metaphor layers.
3 Gerald Midgley lists things to keep in mind to ensure that any project remains ethical.
4 Structural violence is violence that is woven into the fabric of the culture. A group or groups become scapegoated to pay the price so those in power do not suffer. Slavery is a good example.
5 Human history has evolved through various social structures, each more complex than the previous one.
6 The face of democracy is changing with challenges like nuclear threat, climate change, and more. We struggle with the loss of a binding story.

Notes

1 See *Demonic Males: Apes and the Origin of Violence* by Richard Wrangham.
2 See *CLA 2.0* by Sohail Inayatullah.
3 Gerald Midgley is selected to represent a whole field within Systems Theory called Critical Systems Theory, including people like C. West Churchman, Robert Flood, Werner Ulrich, Michael Jackson, and Peter Checkland.
4 See *Selections from the Prison Notebooks of Antonio Gramsci* by Q. Hoare and G. Smith.

5 See *Cultural Violence* by John Galtung.
6 See *The Dawn of Everything* by David Graeber and David Wengrow.
7 Sam Bowles from the Santa Fe Institute determined that often the nutritional value of food decreased after shifting to agriculture.
8 See *An Old New Zealander: or Te Rauparaha, Napolean of the South* by Thomas Buick.

Bibliography

Bowles, S. (2009). *The Emergence of Inequality and Hierarchy: A Network Explanation.* https://sites.santafe.edu/~bowles/NetworkExplanation.pdf

Buick, T. (2009). *An Old New Zealander: Or Te Rauparaha, The Napoleon Of The South* (Rare reprint). Kessinger Publishing. https://www.amazon.com/Old-New-Zealander-Rauparaha-Napoleon/dp/1437487963

Checkland, P. (1999). *Systems Thinking, Systems Practice.* Wiley. http://www.amazon.com/Systems-Thinking-Practice-Includes-Retrospective/dp/0471986062

Churchman, C. W. (1967). Wicked Problems. *Management Science, 14*(4), 141–142. https://doi.org/10.1366/000370209787169876

Churchman, C. W. (1970). Operations Research as a Profession. *Management Sciences, 17*(2), B37–53.

Dostoyevsky, F. (2002). *The Brothers Karamazov.* Farrar, Strauss and Giraux.

Galtung, J. (1990). Cultural Violence. *Journal of Peace Research, 27*(3), 291–305. https://doi.org/10.1177/0022343390027003005

Graeber, D., & Wengrow, D. (2021). *The Dawn of Everything: A New History of Humanity.* Farrar, Straus and Giroux. https://www.amazon.com/Dawn-Everything-New-History-Humanity/dp/B08TYBMHGV/ref=sr_1_1?crid=1CAKCD8D52TT0&keywords=graeber&qid=1650243889&s=books&sprefix=graeber%2Cstripbooks-intl-ship%2C412&sr=1-1

Hoare, Q., & Smith, G. (1992). *Selections from the Prison Notebooks of Antonio Gramsci* (11th print). International Publishers.

Inayatullah, S. (2005). Causal Layered Analysis – Deepening the Future. In *Questioning the Future: Methods and Tools for Organizational and Societal Transformation* (Issue 1). Tamkang University Press.

Inayatullah, S., & Milojevic, I. (2015). *CLA 2.0: Transformative Research in Theory and Practice* (S. Inayatullah & I. Milojevic, Eds.). Tamkang University Press.

Jackson, M. C. (2003). *Systems Thinking: Creative Holism for Managers.* John Wiley & Sons Ltd.

Meadows, D. H. (2008). *Thinking in Systems* (D. Wright & C. Labrie, Eds.). Chelsea Green Publishing Company.

Midgley, G. (2000). *Systemic Intervention: Philosophy, Methodology, and Practice.* Kluwer Academic/Plenum Publishers. https://books.google.com/books?id=TdhElgdyvMAC&pgis=1

Midgley, G., & Pinzón, L. A. (2011). Boundary Critique and its Implications for Conflict Prevention. *Journal of the Operational Research Society, 62*(8), 1543–1554. https://doi.org/10.1057/jors.2010.76

Midgley, G., Munlo, I., & Brown, M. (1998). The Theory and Practice of Boundary Critique: Developing Housing Services for Older People. *The Journal of the Operational Research Society Journal of the Operational Research Society, 49*(49), 467–478. https://doi.org/10.1057/palgrave.jors.2600531

Nietzsche, F. (2021). *Human: All Too Human*. Arcturus.

Peterson, D., & Wrangham, R. W. (1997). *Demonic Males: Apes and the Origins of Human Violence*. Mariner Books. http://www.amazon.com/Demonic-Males-Origins-Human-Violence/dp/0395877431

Ulrich, W. (2002). Boundary Critique. In H. G. Daellenbach & R. Flood (Eds.), *Informed Student Guide in the Management Sciences* (p. 41). Thomson Learning. http://wulrich.com/downloads/ulrich_2002a.pdf

Ulrich, W., & Reynolds, M. (2010). *Critical Systems Heuristics*. Springer.

Wrangham, R. (2019). *The Goodness Paradox: The Strange Relationship between Virtue and Violence in Human Evolution*. Pantheon.

Chapter 10

Reconnecting

Introduction

The first part of this chapter investigates the present global context and looks at possible futures. We have completed our journey from the first living cell to our global society. It is time to pull the threads together to point to pathways to the future. We consolidate our wisdom and put the new understandings, tools and techniques into practice for the benefit of both ourselves and those around us. It is not a clear and straight, linear pathway; rather, we enter a maze to navigate as best we can with what we have available.

We Live in a Troubled World

Our focus has been on understanding ourselves as individual human beings and then how we act in smaller social settings. We live in a global society that is deeply disconnected and rife with abuse and violence. One part of our individual violence arises from how we are immersed in a global cultural rule set that values profit over human well-being. We live in precarious times, and we all need to play our part in enhancing well-being.

In previous times, we had a clear narrative to guide our lives and maintain social cohesion. It moved from tribal gods to one God, to science. Then we began to realise how we can be manipulated and controlled by those controlling the narrative. No single narrative is the truth; all are tainted. Now we have no story to bind us together. This has left a void that John Vervaeke[1] calls *The Meaning Crisis*.

Into the void came the neo-liberal story that the world is made up of separate parts, and that all of these parts are given a monetary value. The global economy is organised so that the wealth flows to the already wealthy, thereby exacerbating inequality. The mass of people pay the price of creating wealth without a fair share. The Earth pays the price of environmental damage.

We have been warned of this since at least the 1970s, and yet have continued headlong towards disaster. It is like the lord of the manor who cannot cover the costs of keeping the household. Staff have been cut to the bare

DOI: 10.4324/9781003533641-10

minimum and now the artwork, the family silver, and the furniture are being sold off. Life may appear to be continuing as normal, but the lord of the manor knows it is only a matter of time before the bank telephones to advise him that the mortgage will be foreclosed. When we reach the point that nature calls in the loan, we will have nowhere else to go.

Nate Hagens[2] writes that we have become energy-blind; that we live in the time of a one-off carbon pulse, where we have access to enormous power through coal, gas, and oil that has enabled civilisation to develop. However, there is a rapidly approaching end to fossil fuels. We create money by pushing a button; at some point, however it must be backed by energy as we spend the money. He foresees a great simplification in our lifestyle as we readjust to the energy levels our world can cope with, and that if we act wisely the transition can be reasonably smooth, but there is every indication that it will be an extremely disruptive time as change is forced on us by our inaction.

While we do not want to drown in the immensity of disconnection, abuse, and violence, we need to understand the global situation to discover ways to cope. At the core of all the threats we face is the story of separateness. Systems wisdom is a story of connecting and disconnecting. Systems is still a young science; it is not the magic pill to fix all ills, but it has a story that reconnects. It is a vital piece in the jigsaw.

The societal level operates through organising. The predominant mode of organisation in government and in business is top-down hierarchies. Power and resources sit at the top, which controls the rest of the system. That is not the only way to organise people and it is not the way hierarchies work in nature. We noted that, as people became increasingly educated and empowered, and new technology emerged, empires gave way to democracies. Today we are witnessing a gigantic increase in technology that increases people's access to information and communication. This enables alternative ways of shared decision-making to be more viable and might even signal a leap to new levels of human functioning.

Peer-to-Peer (P2P) Networks

We know that any human organisation of any size at all needs to form hierarchies in order to manage entropy. It is possible to organise human life so the negative impacts of hierarchies is less prevalent. Peer-to-peer (P2P) networks[3] describe groups that operate directly with each other rather than through a top-down controlling structure. Peer-to-peer actively seeks to involve as many people as possible in the organisation and reduce inequalities. They include co-operatives, open-source organisations, heart-sharing circles, bitcoin, and more.

Michel Bauwens spearheads the peer-to-peer network and notes that P2P networks have three main attributes. First is "peer production", where autonomous individuals come together to create a common resource as in the case of open-source software. Secondly, P2P networks have "peer governance", where the group governs itself through the process of creating resources, and, finally, P2P networks have "peer property", where the resources generated are held in a creative commons. The individual or group creating the resources is given full attribution, but the resources are openly available for all.

Not all tasks would be suitable for a P2P structure. Surgery or piloting a jetliner need control-and-command structures to respond quickly, but many other hospital or airline tasks could operate on a peer-to-peer basis. Peer-to-peer organisations also have their pitfalls, however. Providing the opportunity for all to be involved can make them slower. Often groups that claim to have no leader simply have invisible leaders, who are even less accountable.

The city of Mondragon in northern Spain has grown from one co-operative, which was established in 1955. Mondragon is virtually entirely run by co-operatives, including a bank, a hospital, and a university. Their co-operatives have turnovers of tens of billions of euros every year and connect a wide international network of cooperative ventures.

Similarly, Joshua Vial started a software company in Wellington, New Zealand that prospered. Instead of setting up a traditional hierarchy, he instituted a network of collaborations with other business owners, which is now called "Enspiral".[4] They created a skills bank and a shared fund to which they all contributed. This formed a springboard for new businesses and projects. These include "Loomio", which is software for shared decision-making by large groups with rounds of voting and four choices of vote: agree, disagree, abstain, and block. A block would only be used a few times in a lifetime. "Co-Budget" collects and allocates funds collectively.

Heart-sharing Circles

I have had a long involvement in heart-sharing circles, particularly as a part of men's groups. They have been an effective tool for bringing balance to my life. Sharing circles operate as peer-to-peer groups. They are mostly small groups of up to ten people, but some grow larger. Some are structured with firm rules; others are more freewheeling. Some groups have a closed membership unless they choose to take on a new member, while others are open to anyone at any time. My group meets for about three hours every fortnight, joining with other local groups in a gathering of 20 to 30 people twice a year. My small group also occasionally has a weekend away, where we get the opportunity to go much deeper than usual.

I am constantly amazed at how quickly a supportive group of genuine people can explore deep topics. The themes that consistently return are relationships, health – including death and illness, career, trauma, and early life experiences. Circles are not therapy groups and do not cope with people who need professional help for mental health or other issues, but I have numerous anecdotes of individuals, and indeed myself, who have found heart-sharing circles to be extremely helpful and play a significant part in their healing journey and in maintaining ongoing emotional health. With our journey through the levels of life complete, we now step back to look at the whole journey and what we have learned about living lives beyond violence.

Lessons for the Future

Some key threads have emerged on our journey to know ourselves and seek ways to live more peaceful and fulfilling lives. Arising from the systems principles inherent in the way life is structured, we note that:

1 Error is inherent in human nature. The world is bigger than we can know and our ability to know is constrained by the capacity of our body and its cognitive abilities. We must make our best assumptions while balancing the need for speed, accuracy, and energy. Living systems that make significant errors lose fitness and can be expelled from their niche.
2 Variety creates both opportunity and conflict. Because we are open to error, when we can't find love, we often make do with power, creating the space for our inherent capacity for violence.
3 When a living system cannot process the energy, matter, or information flowing through, or project it out into the world, it remains in the system as a toxic element. We become overwhelmed and often drop a layer of functioning on the Tree of Life. The physical level is the lowest level where we resort to physical violence.
4 Living systems function at many levels, all of which must remain viable. They must provide sufficient mutual support between levels to maintain the overall integrity of the system. Conflict arises when the rules sets of subsystems, whole systems, or supersystems clash. The balance of autonomy and connectivity must be resolved at every boundary. Violence is the invasion of a boundary or the disruption of a flow across a boundary.
5 As a response to unmanaged entropy, living systems create a hierarchy of co-ordinator and management levels and more, if necessary, that contain the entropy but increase inequality that again creates conflict to be resolved., Peer-to-peer organisational structures aim to reduce the impact of inequality.
6 Living systems create mapping systems to map themselves and their environment to make sense of events and enable the system to know what to do. Changing the map is bio-energetically expensive and a risk in case it makes an error. Life tends to resist changing the model often, even when it would be beneficial or even critically necessary to its ongoing functioning.

7 People must align their cognitive mapping with that of other people in their culture, so communication and collaboration are possible. This creates a dominant narrative. Like the personal belief system of a person, it will have errors that lead to structural violence and oppression. The problem of our age is a lack of a cohesive connecting narrative.
8 Every action of a primary system opens the space for a shadow reaction. The shadow system has its own rule set and its own vision. Healthy interactions between the primary system and the shadow system can lead to innovation; all too often, however, it leads to conflict and violence.

Summary of Tools and Techniques

Table 10.1 summarises the skills and techniques mentioned in this book which can be used to live our lives in better ways. They help us build better relationships with the people around us and reduce the temptation to fall back into abuse or violent behaviours towards ourselves and others.

The Spiritual Level

Our journey has taken us from the life level to the mind to the cultural. As digital technology grows, we are undergoing social changes no less significant than the invention of the printing press, which might suggest that a leap to a new level of spiritual development might be possible. The *Dynamics of Life* model provides a framework to explore this shift and some of the challenges we must take on if we are to actualise them in our lives.

Today's enormous range of spiritual beliefs makes it difficult to formulate the *Dynamics of Life* model at the spiritual level. Figure 10.1 might provide a starting point. For some a concept of God is central, while this is not the case for others. Others might use the concepts of soul and spirit. For some, hell is a real place; for others, it is a psychological construct. Perhaps one uniting idea is that we as human beings are part of a wider universe of being that we can come to know and experience, and which enables us to feel more complete in ourselves. It is a direct knowing of our connectedness.

One important part of the spiritual journey is coming to terms with that darker side of our being. We have feared and avoided embracing the fullness of who we are because it is uncomfortable, but it is a necessary part of the journey. Peace is not so much an idyllic state of being we work towards as it is the journey of becoming. It is about accepting responsibility for our darker sides and not projecting them elsewhere, only to perpetuate violence. It is opening a dialogue with our other to explore new possibilities that create healthy ways of resolving difference.

Our disconnected lifestyle has split us from ourselves, others, and our world, creating consequences for many years to come. We are, however, not trapped in our dystopic vision of death and destruction. We can still reconnect to find our wholeness individually, as people, and as a planet.

Table 10.1 A summary of tools and techniques for reducing abuse and violence

	Feedback	Boundary	Awareness	Shadow	Flow	Rule set	Connecting
Techniques that combine levels		Perspective taking Identify stakeholders	Mindfulness Tai chi Yoga Breathing techniques Whare Tapa Whā	Psychosynthesis			
Spiritual	Prayer or meditation	Rituals of protection	Meditation Warm data	Dark archetypal forces	Living in unity in the flow of chi	Good living, religious or spiritual text	Uniting self
Social	Open discussion Acknowledge error Other perspectives	Identify stakeholders	CLA Futures planning	Mediation collaboration with others	Good group processes	Constitution, policy	Organise and work together Peer to peer co-operatives
Thinking	Reflective thinking	Lear statement of boundaries	Values cards	Correcting core beliefs	Rational thinking	Reflect on values and beliefs	Dialogue
Emotional	Empathy – Feel for other Self-awareness	Emotional resilience distress tolerance	1–10 scale Time out Distress tolerance Distraction	Forgiveness Emotional release	Healthy expression of emotion	Emotional Awareness	Emotional vulnerability
Biological	Mine and other body's reaction.	Bodily boundaries	Body scanning	Bodywork massage	Fitness Nutrition	The body	Chemical and electrical messaging

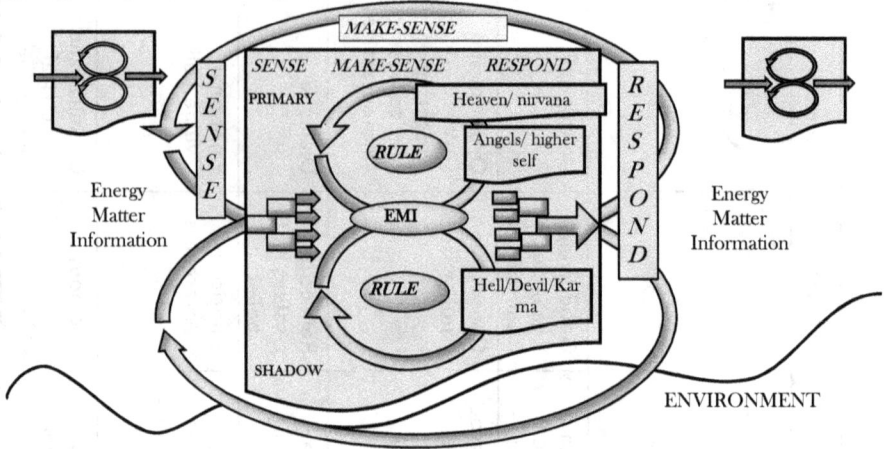

Figure 10.1 The *Dynamics of Life* model at the spiritual level.

As science gains a better understanding of our world, it opens the door to expanding our spiritual awareness of who we are and the many paradoxes inherent in our being. There is a fast-growing body of knowledge of how our brain works and the nature of social interactions that can be even better understood when it is integrated into a systems approach.

Systems wisdom opens the possibility of envisioning a new world based on a rigorous science but embracing the fundamental connectedness of all people and the natural environment. It teaches us to consider other perspectives, seek out the bigger picture, explore relationships between parts, and recognise leverage points. It teaches us to acknowledge and embody the ongoing tensions that create life. We then see seeming opposites as complementary forces to be resolved. We are not hostage to our human nature. If we truly embrace who we are, the pathway to reconnecting back to ourselves, to others, and to the world we live in, opens up. Systems wisdom speaks a narrative of connectedness that can bring us together in nourishing and healing ways, fit for the age in which we live, and take us into the future in wholesome, nurturing ways.

Key Points

1 We live in a world which is facing many dire issues. Systems wisdom has a contribution to making a better world.
2 Peer-to-peer networks can organise groups to be more equal and fair, providing a greater sense of ownership for all involved. They have their weaknesses but are a proven alternative at all scales. Heart-sharing circles are one example of this.
3 Our human nature leaves us vulnerable to falling back into violent ways, but we can choose new and better ways to resolve conflict.

4 Systems wisdom provides a pathway for reconnecting ourselves to our-selves, each other, and the world about us.

5 We are not hostage to our nature. If we use what we have available to us we can create a life beyond violence and abuse.

Notes

1 Watch John Vervaeke's YouTube series *Awakening from the Meaning Crisis*.
2 *See* https://www.youtube.com/@thegreatsimplification.
3 *See* https://wiki.p2pfoundation.net/Michel_Bauwens.
4 See https://www.enspiral.com/.

Bibliography

Bauwens, M. (2005). Peer to Peer and Human Evolution. Integral Visioning. http://62.210.98.10/IMG/P2PandHumanEvolV2.pdf

Bauwens, M. (2006). The Political Economy of Peer Production. *Post-Autistic Economics Review*, 37, 33–44.

Bauwens, M. (2007a). The Next Buddha will be a Collective: Spiritual Expression in the Peer to Peer era. *Revision*, 29(4), 34–45.

Bauwens, M. (2007b). The Peer to Peer Revolution. *Renewal*, 15(4), 25–37.

Pazaitis, A., Kostakis, V., & Bauwens, M. (2017). Digital Economy and the Rise of Open Cooperativism: The Case of the Enspiral Network. *Transfer: European Review of Labour and Research*, 23(2), 177–192. https://doi.org/10.1177/1024258916683865

Ramos, J. M., Bauwens, M., & Kostakis, V. (2016). P2P and Planetary Futures. In R. Carson (Ed.), *Critical Posthumanism and Planetary Futures*. Springer.

Vervaeke, J. (2019). Awakening from the Meaning Crisis. Youtube Video Series. youtube.com/watch?v=5418_ewcOIY

Vervaeke, J. (2020, May). Diagnosing the Current Age: A Symptomology of the Meaning Crisis. https://thesideview.co/journal/diagnosing-the-current-age/

Appendix

These values cards have been developed for use in the field of Family Violence and are centred in New Zealand. They could be adapted to fit other client groups. They can be useful just as cards to open discussions for people to explore different aspects of their being.

Men's Values Cards

A good attitude changes everything
Always do your share
An eye for an eye
Back up your mates
Be fair
Be first to apologise
Be generous
Be loyal
Be positive
Do your best
Don't back down
Don't be greedy
Don't give up
Don't hit women
Don't hold grudges
Don't judge others
Don't trust anyone
Everyone has something to teach me
Everyone is basically good
Everyone is equal
Everyone makes mistakes
Family comes first
Family just let you down
Gays are evil
God will take care of me

Have compassion for other people's suffering
Have gratitude for everything
Have respect for others
Hit first
Honesty is the best policy
I always get what I want
I am always right
I am loved
I am not worthy
I can achieve anything
I can always improve
I can make a difference
I don't care what other people think
I don't let people push me around
I expect loyalty
I know what I am doing
I like to be the centre of attention
I say it like it is
I was never wanted
I'll never amount to anything
I'm not perfect but I try
It's a dog-eat-dog world
It's OK to hit someone if they deserve it.
Keep your word
Ladies first
Life gets better
Life is hard
Life is not fair
Live it up. You only live once
Look after number one
Love makes the world go round
Man is the head of the house
Māoris are lazy
Men don't cry
Money is everything
Never admit you are wrong
Nothing ever works for me
Obey the rules
One law for the rich, another for the poor
Payback feels good
People always do their best
People don't give me a chance
People don't like me
People have to take me as I am

People shouldn't mess with me
Respect your elders
Rules are made to be broken
Some people deserve to die
Some people just need a beating
Take responsibility for yourself
The courts are against men
The system is out to get me
The universe provides for my needs
There's no point trying
Treat others as you would like to be treated
Trust your mates
Weak people get what they deserve
What goes around comes around
Women are bitches
Women are too emotional
Women just let you down
Women rule the world
You are either a man or a woman
You can always help someone
You gotta be staunch
You have to be willing to sacrifice yourself for others
You have to earn my respect
You have to take a risk sometimes
You should forgive people

Women's Values Cards

A good attitude changes everything
Always do your share
An eye for an eye
Back up your mates
Be fair
Be first to apologise
Be generous
Be loyal
Be positive
Do your best
Don't back down
Don't be greedy
Don't give up
Don't hit women
Don't hold grudges
Don't judge others

Don't trust anyone
Everyone has something to teach me
Everyone is basically good
Everyone is equal
Everyone makes mistakes
Family comes first
Family just let you down
Gays are evil
God will take care of me
Have compassion for other people's suffering
Have gratitude for everything
Have respect for others
Hit first
Honesty is the best policy
I always get what I want
I am always right
I am loved
I am not worthy
I can achieve anything
I can always improve
I can make a difference
I don't care what other people think
I don't let people push me around
I expect loyalty
I know what I am doing
I like to be the centre of attention
I say it like it is
I was never wanted
I'll never amount to anything
I'm not perfect but I try
It's a dog-eat-dog world
It's OK to hit someone if they deserve it.
Keep your word
Ladies first
Life gets better
Life is hard
Life is not fair
Live it up. You only live once
Look after number one
Love makes the world go round
Man is the head of the house
Māoris are lazy
Men don't cry
Men are bastards

Men just let you down
Men rule the world
Money is everything
Never admit you are wrong
Nothing ever works for me
Obey the rules
One law for the rich, another for the poor
Payback feels good
People always do their best
People don't give me a chance
People don't like me
People have to take me as I am
People shouldn't mess with me
Respect your elders
Rules are made to be broken
Some people deserve to die
Some people just need a beating
Take responsibility for yourself
The courts are against women
The system is out to get me
The universe provides for my needs
There's no point trying
Treat others as you would like to be treated
Trust your mates
Weak people get what they deserve
What goes around comes around
Women are too emotional
You can always help someone
You gotta be staunch
You have to be willing to sacrifice yourself for others
You have to earn my respect
You have to take a risk sometimes
You should forgive people

Glossary

4e cognition   4e cognition proposes that cognition is enactive, embodied, embedded, and extended. Cognition occurs not only in the brain but also in the body, and even extends out into the world. We find out if a nut fits on a bolt by trying it out in the world, not by thinking about it in our brain.

Autonomy   The ability to act independently without undue influence from other systems or parts. An autonomous system can make its own decisions and act on them. Increasing autonomy generally means a reduction in connectivity.

Autopoiesis   The property of a living system that allows it to maintain and renew itself by regulating its composition and conserving its boundaries by exploiting flows of energy, matter, and information. Luhmann and others also call organisations and other non-biological systems autopoietic, which instead utilise a flow of communications.

Bifurcation   The point where a system must choose between two possible states. To divide out or branch out in two directions.

Causal Layered Analysis   A multi-layered approach to analysing any social situation from four levels – a litany (everyday) level, a systems level, a worldview level, and a myth/metaphor level – which helps maintain a wider perspective on whatever you wish to study.

Chaos   The common usage of chaos is total disorder, where everything is random and there is no predictability. A chaotic system, however, has some connections between the parts, such as the weather or a fire. While general patterns can be discerned, mostly in the short term, no precise predictions can be made with any certainty.

Cognition   The process of acquiring knowledge and understanding through thought, experience, and the senses. It requires sensing, making sense, and responding. 4e cognition widens this by claiming cognition is embedded, enactive, embodied, and extended.

Complex Adaptive System   A complex system that can change its state within its boundary to maintain its existence. It can adapt to changing circumstances. All living systems are complex adaptive systems.

Complex System   A collection of parts that are linked such that the interactions between the parts make them intrinsically difficult to model. They often create unintended consequences. A complex adaptive system is a special type that has more predictability because of constraints placed on the parts.

Complexity Theory   The study of non-linear systems that cannot be readily predicted, especially living and social systems. The key to understanding them is through their organisation.

Connectivity   The ability of the parts of a complex system to connect together for greater benefit. It is complementary to autonomy, where the focus is internal.

Critical System Theory   A branch of Systems Theory that focuses on ethics and morals. They look at how systems can be an emancipatory tool and guard against systems being perverted for nefarious reasons.

Cybernetics   The science of communications and automatic control systems in machines and living things. It arose after World War II. Second-order cybernetics focuses on recognising that an observer of a system is a part of the system.

Cynefin   The system, invented by Dave Snowden using the name Cynefin, which is Welsh for habitat, or the place that is home and welcoming. It cotes five domains of systems: simple/obvious, complicated, chaotic, complex, and disorder. His system includes many other concepts and ideas.

Dissipative system   A dissipative system dissipates energy, creating a flow of energy through the system. All living systems are dissipative.

DSRP   A model created by Derek and Laura Cabrera, recognising that all complex systems create distinctions that form boundaries, operate as integrated systems, form relationships between the parts, and have parts with distinct perspectives.

Energy   Energy creates the capacity to do work. Energy moves through living systems that extract the free energy to change themselves to maintain their existence and do work in the world.

Entropy   The tendency for everything to wear down over time. Entropy is a measure of the disorder or chaos, so entropy always increases over time. Living systems manage entropy to extract free energy to do work. When the living system and the environment are measured, entropy still increases overall, even though the living system creates order within itself.

Exponential growth   This is usually used to describe rapid and increasing growth. In mathematics, it describes growth as described by an exponent (10^x). If x is more than one, there is rapid growth; if x is less than 1, then growth decreases as exponential decay.

Feedback   Feedback occurs when the output of a system becomes the input of that system. If the output is the same as the input, there is no change. Positive feedback leads to exponential growth and negative feedback keeps a system in the same state.

Fractal   Fractals are patterns that are self-similar across scales, which means no matter what level you look at the pattern looks similar. The shape of a small twig is similar to the shape of the whole tree; a little floret of cauliflower is like the whole cauliflower. The proportional change between levels stays the same.

Free energy   The amount of energy available for use. Some energy is always lost as we use it. Some energy is lost as heat.

Hierarchy   The layers in a living system. Organisations typically have a hierarchical structure in which the higher level can constrain lower levels to meet the needs of the higher level. A hierarchy looks a bit like Russian dolls with levels inside levels.

Hierarchy Theory   A theory that looks at how levels of a hierarchy arise and how issues of scale matter. As I focus on one level, I lose focus on others. We can't see the forest for the trees. The theory was principally originated by Tim Allen.

Information   Information is processed, organised, and structured data. Data that is presented in a usable way is information. Information can take on meaning to become knowledge, and can then become wisdom.

Matter   Physical substance that occupies space and time and has mass.

Maximum power principle   The maximum power principle explored by Howard Odum says living systems function to maximise their use of energy. Living systems that maximise their energy gain fitness in their environment and are more likely to survive.

Memory   The ability to collect, store, and retain information for later retrieval.

Negative feedback loop   A negative feedback loop operates to keep a system in the same state over time. An example is a thermostat that operates to keep the temperature in a room constant. When it is too cold, a heater is turned on; when it is too hot, the heater turns off.

Order   The result of constraints placed on the parts of a system to behave in a particular way.

Other   That which is outside the boundary of a living system, especially other living systems. Because we tend to focus on what is inside a boundary, the "other" often leads to suspicion, oppression, or a lack of recognition.

Positive feedback loop   A feedback loop in which the system increases or decreases increasingly like population growth or a loss of monetary value. In practice, increasing positive feedback loops become constrained by a negative feedback loop and level off.

Recursive A recursive process is one in which each response triggers a response from another living system, which in turn triggers yet another response like a game of ping-pong. I respond to your response to my response to your response etc. Conversations are recursive. What I say depends on what you say, that depends on what I say.

Rule set A rule by which parts in a system are constrained in how they act. This might include the action of a DNA molecule, a hormone triggering a body change, a club rule, or a national law.

Sense, make-sense, and respond All living systems must sense, make sense, and respond to know what to do to survive and maintain well-being. They collect data from inside themselves and outside, recognise patterns to make sense and then carry out the appropriate action.

System of systems Living systems are typically comprised of subsystems and are parts of a larger supersystem, so they are nested inside each other like a Russian doll.

Systems Theory The scientific study of systems and how they operate in the world. There are patterns between seemingly very different systems that follow the same functional patterns (isomorphy). The systems sciences explore how things connect and disconnect.

Systems wisdom A term used by the author to describe systems as a way of experiencing the world rather than just a scientific study.

The second law of thermodynamics The second law of thermodynamics states that the universe moves steadily towards a state of disorder or entropy. Energy is increasingly lost over time. Life seems to break the rule and increase order, but if you consider a living system and its environment holistically, the second law remains true.

Values That which a living system deems to be important and guide its action towards its purpose for being.

Viable Systems Model Stafford Beer formulated the Viable Systems Model based on the human body, but it is more commonly used in the area of business management. It proposes that each viable system is comprised of five viable subsystems. One does the work the system is designed for, another provides the support for that system, another monitors progress, another is focused on the outside environment and the final system sets policy and rules.

Warm data A term used by Mora Bateson to describe value data used by living systems that goes beyond the cold scientific facts. Warm data often provides the context for understanding the data.

Acronyms

ACT	Acceptance and Commitment Theory
CAS	Complex Adaptive System
CBT	Cognitive Behaviour Theory
CLA	Causal Layered Analysis
CST	Critical Systems Theory
DBT	Dialectic Behaviour Theory
DoL	Dynamics of Life
DSRP	Distinctions, Systems, Relationships, and Perspectives
P2P	Peer-to-peer
TA	Transactional Analysis
VSM	Viable Systems Model

Index

For Product Safety Concerns and Information please contact our EU
representative GPSR@taylorandfrancis.com
Taylor & Francis Verlag GmbH, Kaufingerstraße 24, 80331 München, Germany

www.ingramcontent.com/pod-product-compliance
Lightning Source LLC
Chambersburg PA
CBHW050607280326
41932CB00016B/2952